BUILD
Confidence

Become Unafraid, Irresistible & Successful

Dr. Stem Sithembile Mahlatini.

Copyright © 2018 Dr. Stem Sithembile Mahlatini.
All rights reserved.

ISBN 978-1-7328275-9-2

All rights reserved. No part of this publication may be reproduced, stored in a retrieval system, or transmitted in any way by any means – electronic, mechanical, photocopy, recording, or otherwise – without the prior permissions of the copyright holder, except by reviewer who may quote brief passages in a review to be printed in magazine newspaper or by radio / TV announcement, as provided by USA copyright law. The author and the publisher will not be held responsible for any errors within the manuscript. All characters appearing in this work are fictitious. Any resemblance to real persons, living or dead is purely coincidental.

Written by: Dr. Stem Sithembile Mahlatini
Drstem14@gmail.com | www.drstemspeaks.com
https://www.drstemmie.com/

Facebook: DrStem Mahlatini **Twitter:** DrStemahlatini
LinkedIn: Drstem Mahlatini **Skype:** Dr.Mahlatini

Foreword by: Dr.Stem Sithembile Mahlatini **Cover Design by:** Masimba Mukundinashe: Ed Pedi Photography Studio & Gardens, North Andover, Massachusetts 01845
978-686-6535 www.edpediphoto.com

Category: Historical, Biographical, Motivational, Inspirational, Educational and Empowerment
Library of Congress Cataloging-in-Publication Data
Printed in the USA

Enjoy the little things in life. For one day you'll look back and realize they were the big things.

DrStem

CONTENTS

INTRODUCTION ... 7

SECTION (1) CONFIDENCE DEFINED ... 15

1. What Is Self Confidence ... 17
2. What Self Confidence Is Not ... 25

SECTION (2) WHY CONFIDENCE MATTERS ... 29

3. Why Confidence Matters: Self Worth ... 31
4. Why Confidence Matters: Self Image ... 41
5. Why Confidence Matters: Relationships ... 55
6. Why Confidence Matters: Careers ... 67
7. Why Confidence Matters: Happiness ... 75

SECTION (3) HOW TO BE CONFIDENT ... 81

8. How To Be Confident: Like Yourself ... 83
9. How To Be Confident: Take Care of Yourself ... 93
10. How To Be Confident: Take Care of Your Body ... 101
11. How To Be Confident: Toss Your Weakness In The Trash and Walk Away ... 109
12. How To Be Confident: Dare To Show You Care ... 119

SECTION (4) WHAT HAPPENS WHEN YOU'RE CONFIDENT   125

13. Self Acceptance **127**

13. Rising To The Challenge Of Setting & Meeting Goals ...**131**

14. Life Looks Good & The Future Looks Bright **135**

15. You Have Control Over Your Emotions **141**

16. Your Education Matters **145**

SECTION (5)   YOUR CONFIDENCE IN ACTION   149

17. Be Confident: Show The World Who You Are **151**

18. Self Confidence Affirmations: **153**

BUILD CONFIDENCE, BECOME UNSTOPPABLE WORKBOOK

Exercise 1: Little Things Matter **159**
Exercise 2: Attitude Is Everything **165**
Exercise 3: There's Power In This Moment **173**
Exercise 4: Everything Starts With Simple Steps **181**
Exercise 5: There's No Such Thing As Failure **187**
Exercise 6: Habits Are Powerful **191**
Exercise 7: You Are Always Learning **197**
Exercise 8: Make Your Dreams Come True **201**

APPENDIX: **213**

INTRODUCTION

Whether you think you can or you can't - you're RIGHT

~Henry Ford

Become Unafraid, Irresistible & Successful

Introduction

According to psychologists, self-esteem and confidence are different. Prof. Richard Petty from Ohio State University, in his interesting TED talk distinguishes them as: Self-esteem is our opinion about ourselves — how much we like ourselves. Confidence is how sure we are of this judgement. However as of this writing and my life experience, I think the two are very close.

While self-esteem is an internal feeling, confidence is its outer manifestation. They are really the two sides of the same coin. Confidence (or lack of it) is usually **quite fluid and can change daily**, even hourly.

Self-confidence may come from a variety of sources which I will be discussing further in this book, -our backgrounds, measuring up to peers, a bad hair day, getting a C on an important test, (which I got a lot of C's in high school), not speaking up when we should. The point is that there is a set of things that matter to us—for instance, our family, our careers, our appearances, etc. Events which affect these, also impact our self-confidence.

Being an introvert is not the cause of one's low self-esteem. Many introverts have healthy confidence. I have learned that ***"Fake it till you make it" is harder to follow than it sounds.***

It's challenging to maintain confident behavior for straight 8 hours at work, every day, unless we hold at least partial belief that the man in the mirror is worth it, self-love, self-assurance is key. We will also talk more about that later.

True confidence follows a model which can be described as ***ABC***: it needs to be based on some actual **Abilities**; we need to **Believe** in these skills, talents or mojos that we have; and confidence is often **Contingent**, yes will depend on various things at the different stages of our lives—for example, one can be confident that they are a good worker, but not so certain in their parenting skills or relationship skills.

Self-confidence is also shaped by our self-perceptions, which, in turn, contain 3 main ingredients—what we think about ourselves, what others think of us, and what we think others think of us. There are 4 main things which further affect our levels of self-esteem—***the 4 Ps***—Perspiration (our attitude toward fear and anxiety), Peers (comparisons to others), Parents (the support we were given by our families), and Performance (academic or career-wise).

Loving and helping others is important—true, but we shouldn't forget that the only constant in our world, our universe is truly ourselves. No one can and will love us more than we can cherish ourselves, no matter what the movies tell us, parents, lovers, or friends tell us. True confidence originates from self-respect.

It starts within us. The whole life process is merely a journey toward re-discovering our own worth as human beings, of what we stand for, and how we want to evolve. It's that simple. We are here to learn how to *not* let our own voice be overcast by the noise of the world.

We all know the necessities of life are water, air (oxygen) and food. Without them we would cease exist. But did you also know that there are a few other things you need in order for your existence to be more than just an existence—one of the most important being self-confidence.

Let me ask you:

- Do you ever feel like you can't take action on some things in your life because you fear being rejected?
- Do you ever feel like you are not someone who could have success in the most important areas in life such as love, friendship, career and health?

- Do you ever feel like no matter how good you perform you are still not good enough?

- Do you ever sabotage for yourself when things are going well for you?

- Do you ever feel deep down like you don't like yourself or that you are bad?

We all have faced these questions at one time or another. I have. I have been there, and it is not a good place to be in. It can feel terribly restricting. I remember vividly my high school years and early college years; my confidence was very low. But this is not something that is set in stone. Low self-confidence is an issue and a challenge but it is something that can be improved greatly upon so that you can feel great about yourself and live your life to its full potential too.

In the 30 plus years I have been in the United Sates, things have changed for me. My confidence is much stronger than when I arrived in the United States of America from my home country of Zimbabwe. And in this book, I want to share what I have learned, what has actually worked and still works to keep my self-confidence up even through rough parts of my days, weeks, months and years.

This book is filled with practical ways you can use to boost your self-confidence. You deserve a healthy self-confidence. In this book you will learn how healthy self -

esteem is about being good to yourself just like you would be good to your best friend. Self-confidence is about expanding your sense of what you deserve in life and not holding yourself back from exploring your full potential.

With healthy self -confidence you can actually start working towards your dreams and stay on that course with the dreams after you have achieved them (instead of self - sabotaging).

I truly believe; You can create any life you want, no matter how difficult it may seem, by understanding how small, positive steps make a difference over time. It's the things you do every day that don't even seem to matter... that do matter the most. At the end of this book I have included a workbook section and that will have question to guide your small steps to becoming confident and unstoppable. I know for sure that Success is the Best confidence Booster ever.

My goal is to instill that same excitement in you, to pursue the very best in you that you don't even know is in you yet, to dream big and achieve those dreams and more. YAY! Good thing is: it is all possible with a healthy self-confidence and mindset. With healthy self-confidence, your mind opens up to new and great expectations and dreams. There is a time for real change. A time for freedom so that you can live the life you really want.

A time to grow and to explore what you want deep down instead of holding yourself back.

Self-confidence...self-worth...self-esteem. Call it whatever you want, but without the ability to like and believe in yourself, not much of anything else really matters in life, because without self-confidence a person does not have the ability or drive to live up to your full potential. And when you aren't living up to your full potential, you are missing out on the best life has to offer you in terms of education, career, relationships and personal time.

Self-confidence isn't always an easy thing to get, though, is it...especially for teenagers and young adults? You are bombarded from every direction; being told how you should dress, what you should look like, how much you should weigh, what sports you should play, what your academic interests should be and on and on it goes. And because most of us don't fit the media and fashion industry's mold of the perfect person, we begin to think less of ourselves when we 'fail' to meet their expectations.

Good new! You don't have to—fit into an unrealistic mold, that is. This book is about helping you discover that it is more than okay to be yourself and how to do so in spite of what the world around you says. So get ready to get real, get personal and get happy with who you are and what you have to offer.

SECTION (1)
CONFIDENCE
DEFINED

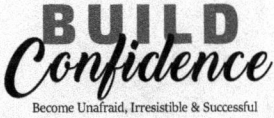

The power to affect your future lies within your own hands.

~Nido Qubein

What Is Self-Confidence

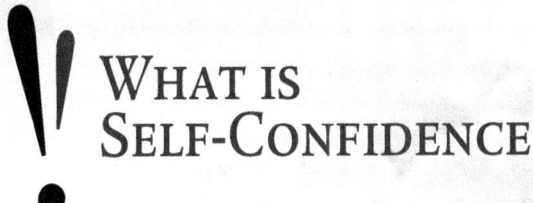

Confidence is defined as being sure and certain of something or someone. It is placing your belief in something or someone for the purpose of directing your thoughts, actions and decisions.

This means that the definition of the word SELF-CONFIDENCE is to be sure and certain of your own personal thoughts, actions and decisions and to allow these thoughts, actions and decisions to be the guiding force of your life.

Okay, so maybe you know what self-confidence *is*, but so what? You also know what DNA is, but you don't have a clue as to how to research and test it, so...

Not everyone needs to know the ins and outs of DNA, but everyone *does* need to know what self-confidence is, what it does and does not look like, how to get it, what to do with it and what to expect as a result of it.

What does self-confidence look like?

A person who is self-confident acts and looks differently than someone whose life is lacking in self-confidence.

The self-confident person has good posture. A person who is confident stands or sits straight and tall. They don't spend time thinking about how they can blend into the room or crowd as if invisible.

The self-confident person has body language to 'prove' it. Body language displaying self-confident includes: making and holding eye contact when speaking to or with someone, keeping your hands at your side or clasped in front or behind you rather than stuffed in your pockets and turning toward the people you are talking to rather than away from them. This is, yes, in addition to standing or sitting straight and tall.

Randy's teacher accused him of lying to her about the reason regarding his tardiness. Randy, knowing he was telling the truth, stood straight and tall, maintaining constant eye contact with the teacher while confidently speaking the truth in spite of her doubts and accusations.

When another teacher finally came to Randy's defense and collaborated his story, she also complimented him on his attitude of confidence and determination.

"I knew I was right," Randy said. "No one should ever back down from the truth—even when the person they are going against is someone in authority."

The self-confident person can laugh at their own mishaps and mistakes. Heather and Dana were confident, vivacious teenagers. They were both great students, but they also loved to laugh and have a good time—even when it included laughing at themselves...

Heather and Maggie were in the lunch line at school one day when they discovered they were in line behind Roger—the guy Heather had a major crush on. Wanting to get his attention and possibly even talk to him, Heather turned around and said something to Maggie she knew Roger would be interested in hearing. She said it just loud enough to make sure Roger heard her.

The 'plan' worked. Roger heard, stopped and tuned around to say something to Heather. Unfortunately, Heather, who was still facing Maggie and walking backwards, did not know that Roger had stopped. When she quickly turned to see what he was doing, she ran into him, which upset her tray and sent her green beans and ham flying through the air and into the milk cooler and all over "Mr. Wonderful".

Now most girls in her situation would have run from the room in tears and red-faced in humiliation. Not Heather and Maggie. The two apologized to Roger (and others in general) while laughing so hard they could hardly contain themselves. Then Heather picked up her tray and said, "Oh well, I wasn't very hungry anyway." Roger, who also took the whole incident with good-natured humor, picked a green bean off his shirt and said, "I am—so thanks for the extra green beans."

Being able to laugh at your own mishaps is important. In doing so you tell yourself and others you know you aren't perfect and that you are more than okay with that.

The self-confident person is neat and clean in their appearance. Well-groomed hair and skin, clothes that are clean, neat and fit well and an overall impression that you take pride in your appearance are indicators of people who care about themselves and who want and expect others to respect and care about them, too.

This is NOT to say you have to have the latest and best in shoes and clothes to be neat and well-groomed. It is also NOT to say that you have to paint on a thick coat of makeup to look your best. It simply means to always put your best self out there for both yourself and others.

Besides, when you look your best, you:
- Ÿ Feel better about yourself
- Ÿ Let others know you are worth respecting
- Ÿ Make a positive impression

The self-confident person takes care of their body. Seventeen year-old Karrie has already been offered full scholarships to three universities because of her musical talent. Any and everyone who hears her sing say she is 'going places' and her ability to play the piano is equally admired. Karrie doesn't get much physical exercise, though, so she is somewhat overweight.

She was self-conscious about it, but not enough to get serious about eating a healthier diet and getting regular exercise. However, when she did not get the leading role in a regional musical production, she was convinced it was because of her weight. Karrie was so distraught that she began purging (vomiting up) everything she ate in an effort to lose weight.

She dropped some weight, but she also passed out while driving to school one morning and ran into a school bus filled with children. Thankfully no one was seriously hurt and Karrie realized she needed to be confident in herself as a person instead of thinking her musical talent was the only thing of value about her.

Getting plenty of exercise, rest and eating a healthy diet allows your body to function as it should...which results in good physical health...which leads to feeling good about yourself...which leads to being self-confident.

The self-confident person doesn't always have to be right or be in control. Being self-confident is about being certain of your ability to form your own feelings, thoughts, opinions and ideas. It is not about forcing these thoughts, ideas and opinions on others or always having to be in control. Being self-confident is being respectful of authority and knowing how to balance that respect with being able to think for yourself.

People who lack self-confidence in their ability to think for themselves end up following a leader into trouble, into uncomfortable situations, into life-changing events…and possibly even to death.

The self-confident person isn't afraid to be afraid. Self-confidence isn't the same as rushing into something without worry or fear of the consequences. Self-confidence isn't about being afraid of something. Self-confidence is trusting in your ability to acknowledge your fear and deal with it maturely and rationally.

Well, what do you think? Now that you have been reminded of what self-confidence looks like, how self-confident would you say you are?

What changes do you feel you need to make in order to become more self-confident?

How would making these changes affect your life?

REMMBER: The self-confident person:
- **Has good posture**
- **Displays confident body language**
- **Can laugh at their own mishaps and mistakes**
- **Is neat and clean with their appearance**
- **Takes care of their body**
- **Doesn't always have to be right or in control**
- **Isn't afraid to be afraid**

Good new! You don't have to—fit into an unrealistic mold, that is. This book is about helping you discover that it is

> Too many people overvalue what they are not and undervalue what they are.
>
> ~Malcolm S. Forbes

What Self-Confidence Is Not

If something goes up it must come down. If something starts it has to end. In other words, everything has an opposite—including self-confidence. In fact, self-confidence has several opposites.

The opposites of self-confidence

Pride and Arrogance: The word pride has both positive and negative meanings. When talking about pride being the opposite of self-confidence, it means to brag about yourself and your abilities and to believe that you are better than other people and to act on these beliefs. Think about it...you do not enjoy being around someone who is always bragging and making themselves the center of attention. So, what makes you think anyone else does, either?

Insecurity: People who are insecure (lack self-confidence) often try to hide this fact by doing things they shouldn't and/or saying things that are not true. They do these things to get attention for the things they do and/or say; hoping no one will notice what they do not like about themselves.

Linda and her family lived in a small town. So when her dad went to prison for robbing a gas station, she and her mom were pointed at, stared at and talked about. Linda was embarrassed, angry and felt like she was being punished for the crime her dad had committed. Knowing how hard it was on both her and her daughter, Linda's mom decided to move them to a new town in order to make a fresh start.

Linda was desperate to keep her family's secret. So to keep people from asking questions about who she was, where she had come from and other questions about her family, Linda created her own version of her life. She told people her dad had been killed in Afghanistan and that they had moved there to get away from all the memories. She told everyone she met at school what a great life she had before—lots of friends, head cheerleader in her old school and that she had lived in three different countries. She also said it made her mom really sad to talk about it and asked that no one bring it up if they were around her.

Peers and teachers had no reason to doubt Linda's story; showing sympathy and going out of their way to make her feel welcome. Linda was thrilled with having reinvented her life and the positive attention she got as a result. But every lie is exposed sooner or later and Linda's lies came crashing down on her when she and her mom saw one of her teachers in the mall. When the teacher told Linda's mom she was sorry for their loss, Linda's mom graciously said "Thank you" and moved on; on to a more private setting where she insisted Linda explain what was going on.

While Linda's mom wanted to spare her daughter any more embarrassment, she knew she could not let her daughter continue to live a lie. She also knew Linda needed to learn that she could be her truly wonderful self without talking about her dad. She explained to Linda that when people asked about her dad all she had to say was that he was not a part of their life. That's all. No further explanation necessary. And if people asked for one, all she had to say was that she did not want to talk about it.

Linda's mom also contacted the teacher to tell her that her husband was not dead, but that he was no longer a part of their lives. She also asked that Linda be allowed to be the one to 'come clean' about the lies she had told.

While Linda didn't make a big announcement, it didn't take long for people to find out she'd been lying about her dad. When one of the people Linda liked most dropped her as a friend, she told Linda it wasn't because her dad had left them—she told her it was because she couldn't trust her not to lie.

Self-confidence is not about never changing your mind. An easy-to-understand example of this is Santa Claus. When you were four, you were most likely of the opinion that Santa was real and had no problem confidently proclaiming your beliefs. Fast-forward to the present. You no longer believe in Santa and are equally confident in saying so as you were when you believed the complete opposite.

Being self-confident does not mean you shouldn't be willing to listen to others and be open to new concepts and ideas and changing your mind to think or feel the same way. It's not about never changing your mind. Self-confidence is changing your mind because YOU feel it is the right thing to do.

Do you see the difference between what confidence is and isn't? As you read through each explanation, did you feel any of them described who you are? If so, do you understand how each of these reflects negatively on your personality? What can you do make positive changes to make you more self-confident?

REMEMBER: Self-confidence is not:

- **Arrogance and pride**
- **Insecurity**
- **Stubbornness**
- **Bullying others**

SECTION (2)
WHY CONFIDENCE MATTERS

You are your own judge. The verdict is up to you.

~Astrid Alauda

Why Confidence Matters: Self-Worth

Knowing what self-confidence is—and isn't—is important. But even more important is knowing why self-confidence matters in life, how to develop a greater sense of self-confidence and what happens when you do.

Why self-confidence matters is a question with more than one answer. While each answer is equally important, the first one we will look at is self-worth.

Self-worth is knowing you are a person of value; that you are deserving of a life of fulfillment and happiness just because you are you. It is having a healthy and positive opinion of yourself.

Devon was born to parents who were ill-equipped to be parents in basically every way. Devon unfortunately was the one who suffered the reality of this via physical, emotional and mental abuse.

Devon is the kind of kid who could easily fall through the cracks and end up in a dead-end job with no chance for a bright future, because the majority of kids like Devon have no self-worth. They believe their abuse and neglect is their fault; that they either did something to deserve it or just aren't special or good enough to be treated the way parents are supposed to treat their kids. Devon, however, is not like most abused kids.

While he did wake up every morning wondering why his parents didn't love him and why they treated him the way they did, he was smart enough to know that it wasn't his fault. By the time he was fifteen, Devon had the respect of his teachers, his peers and other adults who knew him.

"I figured if everyone else could see I wasn't a screw-up, then I wasn't. It took a while, but I finally got to the point when I didn't care what my parents said or did because I know I deserve better and thanks to people who believed in me and loved me, I have it."

The degree of self-worth you have determines how confident you are in showing and expressing the real you. You cannot have one without the other. Self-worth isn't always an easy quality to have and develop, though—especially with all the tugging and pulling on your mind and emotions from the media, peers, parents, teachers and the world in general.

While self-worth is something that comes from within, it is the result of outside 'forces'; forces that include:

A sense of security. While not everyone is fortunate enough to live in a home they feel emotionally or physical safe and secure in, it is essential to have someone and someplace to call your safe place. Everyone needs to know they have someone and someplace they can go to without fear of being ridiculed, harassed or abused.

A sense of validation. To know your thoughts and opinions matter to someone is essential for one's sense of self-worth. A child's need to receive affirmation that they made good choices or did something correctly is just the beginning—but oh, what an important beginning it is. From there, a child seeks validation from their teachers, their peers, their spouse and their boss. To receive little or no validation for your thoughts, ideas and efforts results in a person who feels totally inadequate and incapable of doing anything on their own.

A sense of value.

Much like being validated, everyone needs to feel valued and loved

The first step in building a sense of self value is to stop comparing yourself to others and evaluating your every move; in other words, you need to challenge your critical inner voice. The critical inner voice is like a nasty coach in our heads that constantly nags us with destructive thoughts towards ourselves or others. This inner dialogue or conversation of critical thoughts or "inner voices" undermines our sense of self-worth and value and even leads to self-destructive behaviors, which make us feel even worse about ourselves.

So here is the something you need to know. We all have a "critical inner voice," which acts like a cruel coach inside our heads that tells us we are worthless or undeserving of happiness.

This coach or inner critical voice is shaped from painful childhood experiences and critical attitudes we were exposed to early in life as well as feelings our parents had about themselves.

While these attitudes can be hurtful, over time, they have become engrained in us. As adults, we may fail to see them as an enemy, instead accepting their destructive point of view as our own.

However, we can change our thoughts, our inner dialogue, one that we call "the inner critic" so that we can begin to see ourselves for who we really are, rather than taking on the inner critic's negative point of view about ourselves.

We actually can differentiate from the ways we were seen in our family of origin and begin to understand and appreciate our own feelings, thoughts, desires and values.

The Inner Critic

Now, what is your inner critic? It is that small or sometimes big voice that stabs or pokes you. It drives you down a downward spiral or negative thought patterns and creates a bad day or week from one small misstep or conversation for example. It is the voice that tells you that you that:

- You are a bad person.
- No one really likes you for who you are.
- You always fail in relationships.
- You aren't good at your job at all and someone will figure that out and throw you out.
- That you are worse or uglier than someone else.
- That you are the one to blame for everything that goes wrong.

Those are just some common examples. The inner critic has a lot of rules and Shoulds that it wants you to live up to. It is not always easy to understand that it is your inner critic, that it is that part of you that is pushing you down.

For many it has become such a normal part of the everyday inner dialogue as you get up in the morning, go to work or school, come home for evening activities and as you lie in bed at night and are going to sleep that you may not react to those inaccurate, distorted and negative statements that you are telling yourself about yourself.

So why do you have this voice inside of your head?

Because it helps you in life. Yes, the inner critic actually helps you. It helps you to achieve things and to stay motivated. It helps you to fit in with the people in your world. It helps you to cope with many situations in life. It helps you to avoid many painful situations. It protects you from fear of failure, fear of success, fear of rejection. It reduces anxiety.

It makes you feel safer and more comfortable. It gives you ways to cope with life. But these ways are not ideal, and you can replace them with better and healthier alternatives at any given moment.

But first let us take a look at the origins of the inner critic.

Where does the voice of the inner critic come from?

Many of the Shoulds and rules that form acceptable behavior in the eyes of the inner critic come from your parents, other people around when you were a kid, friends, media and society. Now, everyone has an inner critic. I do too. It isn't something that you can magically eliminate.

But you can learn to manage your inner critic much better, so it does not cause many problems at all. You can take back control over your life and disarm that inner voice as soon as it pops up instead of letting it walk right over you and restrict your journey in life.

Some examples of self-critical thoughts could be:

- Damn, late for work again, I'm so sloppy.

- Wow, she looks cool. But someone like that would never like me.

- I'll probably not do well on the presentation this afternoon.

-

Defusing Your Inner Critic

There are three parts to defusing your inner critic:

1. Discovering the themes of your own critic. You do this by keeping a thought journal for a day or more of what is going on in your day, what you are thinking, what you are saying to yourself. Take time to analyze the notes you take in that journal.

2. Talking back to your critic. You can literally talk back to your self-critic when you find yourself having thoughts feelings as in examples above.

3. Replacing the inner critic with something better.

How do you then silence your inner critic:

. 1. Saying Stop!

Whenever I get a negative and self-critical thought in my head one of the first things I often do is to say this in my own head: Stop! Or I say to myself: "No, no, no, we are not going there!". Then I immediately redirect my thoughts and focus on something more positive. My sisters always say I am extra with the positivity. The good thing about me controlling my inner critic is, I am able to remain calm and be positive. You can do the same when your inner critic pipes up and starts to want to drag you down or keep you on track with its own methods.

When you have the self-critical thought that you suck or that you will never pass the test in school use your own stop-word or phrase as quickly as you can. In your mind, say or shout: Stop! Or tell yourself something that makes your thoughts stop and helps you to interrupt this thought pattern before it grows into more thoughts and you get lost in a negative funk for the rest of the afternoon. Some people often use the statement: "No, no, no, we are not going there!" Some people say using: "No, that is just stupid" statement to stop their inner critic in its tracks works magic.

So for example, if you failed a test; stop the critical thinking by saying to yourself " I failed the test this time. But I am still good as a person and by studying better for the retest I am likely to pass it." It will take some time for the habit to stick but that is OK. Do the best you can, try to use your stop-phrase or word as often as you can and you will discover that after a while your mind may start to say it almost automatically when the critic pops up.

REMEMBER: Self-worth...
- Comes from within your heart—believing and knowing you matter just because
- Gives you the ability to express yourself
- Gives you the ability to think for yourself
- Needs outside 'forces' in order to grow and thrive
    - o Sense of security
    - o Sense of validation
    - o Sense of value (unconditional love)

> Work on being in love with the person in the mirror who has been through so much but is still standing

~ (Unknown)

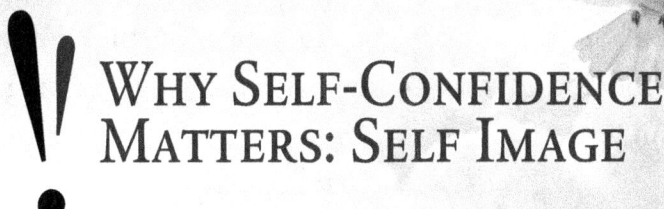

Why Self-Confidence Matters: Self Image

Discovering Your Worth and True Self-Image

In this section lets take a look at two very important things to keep a healthy sense of self-confidence.

The first thing is the unconditional worth that you have. This unconditional worth is something that cannot be compared or decreased. This is a worth that we all have as human being no matter what we have achieved or not achieved. It is your inner core of worth that is unchanging.

The second thing we will look at is how to find a more accurate image of yourself, your core worth and the outer part of your self-confidence such as your skills and achievements. If you have low self-confidence it is very easy to start underestimating yourself and to have a negatively distorted image of who you are and what you can do.

Your inner core of worth.

Maybe the most common way to derive self-confidence

today is to do it through achievement. You do good and someone – mom or dad, teacher, boss, partner, friends, media – tell you that you are good and have worth. I don't think that there is anything wrong with focusing on doing the right thing.

But problems occur when you do what someone else thinks is the right thing (instead of doing what you deep down feel is right). And problems do pop up when you base your whole self-worth on just your accomplishments. Such worth is based on various conditions (such as you accomplishing something or not). And then life and your self-esteem become more of a rollercoaster and something that is controlled by others than it needs to be.

No, things don't have to be that way. Because there is another part of self-confidence that you get the day you are born and this is with you unchanging throughout your life. It is your inner core of worth. Where does it come from? Well, it already here even though you may not think of it that way. You see, you already have a worth because you are here. You have been born into this world, you are alive here and now and you are an everyday miracle. Because of that you have a worth that is always there as long as you are here.

I am excited for you to be learning about this now because it is time to rediscover and reclaim this core self-worth and self-confidence from your own bad habits, critical thoughts and outside forces that may have made you forget, neglect or de-value this important part of your worth. You are a magnificent creation. So unique that there is NO ONE like you now or ever. You are one of a kind YOU. So many things have had to go right and work together for you to exist. All your inner workings – your mind and all the cells and parts of your body – work in unison every day. You have the ability to learn new things and discover new parts of your world, create whatever you put your mind to, get whatever you decide you want to get and create a new you at any given day

Guess what:

No one can see the world from your perspective.

No one has exactly the same way of thinking.

No one else has exactly your sense of humor or the combination of things you love or dislike.

There is no one quite like you among the 7 billion people in the world. And there has never been or will be either. This is true for everyone that are here now. And that is why we never can become worthless.

Even though you may fail and feel bad about yourself your core of unconditional worth is still there inside of you. Even though you have failed with one thing your body and mind still goes on. You still see things from your perspective, think your odd and awesome thoughts and laugh at the things you find funny. You are still you to the core. And no one or nothing can take your core worth away.

Keeping this notion that you are unique in mind will boost your confidence when faced with moments of low self-worth or low self-confidence. Whenever you feel bad about yourself or your mood is low, remember that you are never worthless as long as you are alive, NEVER.

Developing a New Perspective and a New Self Image

Let me ask you:

When you look at yourself, what do you see?

Do you see yourself just the way you are?

Probably not. I don't think anyone does. We filter the world and even our image of ourselves through our mind and thoughts. The view of ourselves is clearly disoriented most times. Some people may have a self-image where they overestimated themselves and think they are much more important than they are.

Others, that are having low self-confidence, may not think very highly about themselves.

Or at least parts of themselves. This image may come from what your parents said and did, what your teachers and kids at school told you, what your friends and partners have let you know over the years.

It also comes from how you choose to look at yourself and choose to accept what you have heard about yourself. This is key because you can change the way you look at yourself and what you choose to define the real you.

Have you ever challenged your self-image, how and what you think of yourself?

Here are some tips to challenge your self-image and create a newer self-image.

1. Stop Worrying about Other People's Opinions

Have you noticed that everyone has an opinion about anyone and everything? So if someone has said or done something to destroy your ego a bit, then remember that's just one person, and there are plenty of others out there cheering you on.

After all, the most important opinion is your own anyway. At all times know that you're doing your best and you can't control what other negative people or person has to say about it.

2. Focus on Your Strengths

People tend to dwell on things they're not good at, or aspects of their appearance they're not happy with. In this distorted state of negativity, it is very easy to forget that you bring a lot to the table – and have talents that some others don't.

"Make a list of all your assets, talents including skills, experiences, physical and social resources, talents, and anything else that makes you feel good about yourself and keep a folded card or paper in your wallet or pocketbook. You're more than one thing; you're many things to many people, so remember that you're dynamic and competent. You are valuable, loved, lovable and capable of becoming much more than you are, if you believe and go after what you want. It is possible.

3. Tackle your Fears

Many people I think underestimate the hold that fear can have in their life. It actually affects the young and old believe it or not. Fear is real is what I always say. I think what I have learned is to Stop and question myself when I don't go through with what I want to, when I don't do well, when I am in doubt, I ask myself "Could this be fear?", because fear will sneak up on you and get in the way of any exciting plan you might have.

So challenge yourself and why not "feel the fear and do whatever you desire to do anyway". When it comes to creating a success filled life you are going to need to develop a fearless mindset and desire to make it, "no matter what".

4. Treat Yourself Like You Would a Best Friend

Negative thoughts can creep into our brains and tell us we're not good enough or confident enough to tackle a particular task, but you can tell that little voice where to go at any time. One way to break this pattern is to ask yourself if you'd talk to your best friend the way you're (unfairly) talking to yourself. If not then you don't deserve to talk yourself down and upset yourself. Be as loving and kind as you would with your best friend.

Another trick is to distract yourself from negativity or negative thinking by being in the moment. Look around, observe the room you're in, take in the smells, be aware of your sense of touch – basically, get into a more meditative state where your mental energy is being redirected away from a dark place.

5. Change your Outer Image

While confidence is something we have within, changing your outward appearance can be helpful to the way you feel and think about yourself. What you look like will always affect your confidence. It is therefore important that you put a little more effort into making sure your outer presentation is fulfilling and make you look and feel good.

Improving your outer image includes getting a new hairstyle, a new and more colorful wardrobe – if you like the person you're looking at in the mirror a little more, it could help you more confidently face your day. If you get some nice comments from friends or strangers, then that's just a bonus! I noticed everyone is startled when they receive an unsolicited compliment, it just makes you feel good that you look good.

6. Straighten your Posture

This may seem a bit weird, but if you're a very unsure person you're probably walking with your shoulders rolled forward and your head down, which doesn't help you feel confident walking down the street (not to mention not doing any favors for your spine and neck).

The way you sit stand can say more than words, be mindful stand and sit straight and sure of yourself. Yes straightening your posture will boost your self-worth and confidence.

7. Use Creative Visualization

Creative visualization is a mental technique that uses the imagination to make dreams and goals come true. ...

Creative visualization uses the power of the mind and is the power behind every success. By visualizing a certain event, situation, or an object, you attract it into your life. This book is a result of my visualizing a best seller book that would help the young and old boost their self-confidence for success, life, career and marriage.

Visualization techniques have been used by successful people to visualize their desired outcomes for ages. The practice has even given some high achievers what seems like super-powers, helping them create their dream lives by accomplishing one goal or task at a time with hyper focus and complete confidence. In fact, we all have this awesome power, but most of us have never been taught to use it effectively. Elite athletes use it. The super-rich use it. And peak performers in all fields now use it. That power is called creative visualization.

The daily practice of visualizing your dreams as already complete can rapidly accelerate your achievement of those dreams, goals, and ambitions. Using visualization techniques to focus on your goals and desires yields four very important benefits.

1.) It activates your creative subconscious mind which will start generating creative ideas to achieve your goal.

2.) It programs your brain so that you are able to be more in tune with recognizing and receiving the resources you will need to achieve your dreams.

3.) It activates the law of attraction, thereby drawing into your life the people, resources, and circumstances you will need to achieve your goals.

4.) It builds your internal motivation to take the necessary actions to achieve your dreams.

A lot of people are not sure whether they can visualize because they fear it could be way too difficult to do. Well guess what? visualization is really quite simple. Let us talk about how.

Create a Vision Board or Goal Vision Board

I love, I mean I really love this technique.

One power visualization technique is to create a photograph or picture of yourself with your goal, as if it were already completed. I know this might sound weird but I am going to ask you to be open to learning this life changing skill. If one of your goals is to own a new car, take your camera down to your local auto dealer and have a picture taken of yourself sitting behind the wheel of your dream car. I had with my BMW and yes I got it. If your goal is to visit Paris, find a picture or poster of the Eiffel Tower and cut out a picture of yourself and place it into the picture, wanted many countries including UK, Russia, Canada and yes I have many more on my vision board which I know I will speak and conduct workshops in. My marriage, my wedding all have been on my vision board for years and I knew I will get here one day.

If you leave in USA or any country with stores that sell poster boards buy a poster board, magazines, color pencils and hold a vision board party where friends or even customers can come and create a vision board with you. It is so much fun and the best part is seeing it all come to pass.

Now all you need to do is Believe and start enjoy living as if you have already achieved those visions you have put on your board.

REMEMBER: Your Dream Life depends on your self-confidence because...

You must have confidence in order to create your dream vision board

You must have confidence to be able to open your mind on what's possible for you .. which everything and anything you want

You must have confidence in order to commit to learn and get all that you need to do to create and live your dream life

You must believe in you, and know that no matter how long it takes, all dreams do come true

You must like and love yourself if you expect others to believe in you and support you, you deserve the best, be the best.

STUDY NOTES

> In the end, who among us does not choose to be a little less right to be a little less lonely

~Robert Brault

Why Self-Confidence Matters: Relationships

We know confidence is being certain and sure of something and of yourself; your abilities, your thoughts and your value as an individual. When you look at that definition, though, it seems a bit me-centered, doesn't it? So what does self-confidence have to do with relationships? Quite a bit, actually.

Before we start looking at the specifics of how and why being confident affects your relationships, let's remind ourselves of what a relationship is. A relationship is a connection between two (or more) people. The very definition of the word answers the question of why and how confidence and relationships are linked. It is the word connection.

To be connected justifiably presumes we will interact, converse, share, communicate, give, take, sacrifice, reciprocate, depend upon, support, encourage and even disagree with someone. That's a lot of connection, isn't it; meaning you need to be confident in who you are, what you have to offer and what you need as a person in order to be able to truly connect and for the relationship to be healthy.

With that being said, let's get down to the business of looking at how and why confidence matters to your relationships.

Confidence lets you enter a relationship. Picture a group of toddlers and preschooler-age children playing together in a room. Little or no thought goes into their interaction. They just do it. Okay, so sometimes it's not pretty when two kids want the same toy at the same time, but even then, both are usually confident enough in who they are to express their desires and opinions.

As we get older, though, things change—more for some than for others. Someone says something to make us feel self-conscious or unworthy to be part of a group or to initiate a friendship. We are fearful of rejection. We lack social skills necessary to know how to approach people.

Whatever the reason, everyone is hit with at least an occasional lack of confidence when it comes to entering into a relationship. That's life. But living with fear, social ineptness, or feelings of inadequacy on a regular basis, is not normal, healthy or necessary.

To gain a greater sense of confidence when it comes to entering a relationship, as yourself why you have trouble entering a relationship, i.e., making friends, talking to people you do not know, etc... Be honest with yourself, because without acknowledging why you *lack* confidence you will never *gain* confidence.

Once you know the reason for your lack of confidence you will be able to take the necessary steps to rebirth the confidence you once had and make new friends, social and business contacts.

I've never been what anyone would describe as shy. I've always made friends easily and have been outgoing. But two and a half years ago we moved to a new town. I've volunteered for things, joined a couple of clubs and put myself out there to meet people. On the surface most people are nice, but overall, I don't feel like I fit in. I've always been pretty confident in who I am, but I'm beginning to think I will never fit in here. I know it's pretty much my responsibility, but I have to admit I'm beginning to feel pretty defeated and unwanted. –Rita

Confidence gives you the strength to say no to relationships. Not all relationships are healthy. There are some relationships you need to walk or even run away from. Many times, though, people lack the strength and courage to get out of these relationships because they lack confidence in their ability or worthiness to do so.

This lack of confidence is exactly what an abuser or one who seeks to control others through mental or emotional mind games wants. They do not encourage those they are controlling to think for themselves, to question the status of the relationship or to believe they deserve better or are capable of doing/having anything better.

One part of being more assertive is to ask for what you want. Another part is to set limits, to say no.

Not being able to say no can becomes something that both stresses you out and lowers your self-esteem. You may feel drained and have no time for yourself after you have done everything everyone wants you to do, you may feel like you are not behind the wheel in your own life but that you almost always working towards someone else's goals. You may even feel used by people and become resentful with bitter taste in your mouth.

Learning to say no doesn't have to be that hard though. By just raising your self-esteem as I mentioned on previous pages you will naturally feel like being treated better by people and you won't accept or tolerate some kinds of requests or behavior. You will become the highest authority in your life. This makes it easier to say no to other people in an assertive way. Now, saying no is not always fun, but you have to be the boss of your life.

You have to make the decisions and say no both to yourself and to others if necessary.

It is essential that you gain the confidence you need to say no to relationships that make you less than who you are. It won't be easy and it will be scary at times. But it will also be worth it in every way and every day for the rest of your life.

I spent the first several years of my life wondering what I had done to make my parents treat me the way they did and trying to do something to make it better. But when I was about eleven or twelve, I realized my teachers and a couple who always took me to church didn't have a problem with who I was. In fact it was just the opposite. They all kept telling me I was a 'good kid' and how proud they were of me. I knew then and there I had a choice to make.

I could believe my parents and continue being mentally and physically abused or I could believe everyone else and do my best in life to be the best me I can be. Today I'm twenty-one, a sergeant in the Marine Corps, married to my high school sweetheart and we have a baby girl who will be one next year. I have no communication with my parents because I now know it is okay to say no to relationships that endanger or kill your confidence. -- Keith

To gain the confidence to say no will require you to see yourself for who you are—not who someone else says you are. It will require you to seek the help and encouragement of those who want to see you thrive and prosper emotionally and mentally even more than you do physically.

Being able to say no isn't just about abuse on any level, though. Being able to say no is something you need to feel confident in saying when your friends, family, boss and co-workers place unrealistic and unfair expectations on you. You need to be confident enough in what you bring to these relationships to be able to say no sometimes without worrying that in doing so you risk losing the relationship.

Confidence in the fact that you are being valued in the relationship and/or bring value to the relationship is what makes it possible for you to say no. If you do not have this, the relationship is not a healthy one and needs to change or be eliminated.

You have the right to ask for what you want and need in life

This is a very important point: you have the right to ask for legitimate needs in your life. Those needs could be physical, emotional, social or of other kinds. You also have the right to ask for what you want in life.

If you feel you have low self-confidence and that you would like to be more assertive then there is also the risk that you underestimate what your legitimate needs are. You might see such a need as simply a want, as a something that would be nice or good to have but not really something that is necessary. And so you might not ask at all. When you ask for something the person you ask has the right to respond or act as he or she wants. But remember, not matter what the response maybe you always have right to ask and how the response makes you feel is all up to you, how you receive it. Be prepared for the no or decline to help you and get what you want so that you don't set yourself up for upset. Other people have the right to help or not help.

As your self-confidence is strengthened, as you for example talk back to the inner critic and as you change your negative thought habits your self-confidence goes up. What's so exciting is your sense of what you deserve in life also goes up. I found that in my life, as my self-confidence went up I was no longer OK with accepting some kinds of behavior from people or less than what I deserve. There were also many moments now when I look back, my confidence dropped and my path changed, my energy changed and failure began to be a daily dose for me.

With my confidence up, it just started became more natural to ask for things because I now felt I deserved to have such things in my life. As your self-confidence goes up it becomes natural to talk back, to say no, to be more assertive to get what you feel you deserve. This is for one of the main reasons why I strive to keep my self-confidence high because then I know I will naturally open myself up to be more assertive and to go for what I feel I deserve. It is very exciting when you realize that and keeping up your work on your self-esteem then becomes even more important to you. Be ready too because many people are very intimidated with confident people, it is ok when people leave you or dismiss you. There will be those who are not intimidated by your greatness who will hang out with you, work with you, help you and have fun with you. Don't settle. Be Encouraged.

You teach people (relationships) by how you behave

As you know, children do as you do, not as you say. This principle works for other people in your life too. People learn about you and your limits from your behavior more than your words.

If you stand up and say no, if you set limits in your life and if you are assertive with what you want and don't want people will pick on your new behavior. And you will encounter less situations where you have to say no or where someone tries to steamroll right over you.

Asking for what you want is something I used to have trouble with. It has become easier as my self-confidence has gone up.

What do you have trouble asking for?

Who do you have trouble asking for something?

Confidence gives you the strength to commit to a relationship. To commit to a relationship involves making the conscious decision to be a giver and taker, a sacrifice and a receiver, a speaker and a listener and a doer and observer.

Without confidence you cannot truly be any of these things. Without confidence you don't feel you have anything worth giving or the belief that you are deserving of taking from someone. You don't have the humility it takes to sacrifice or receive. Without confidence you do not have the courage to speak up or the ability to listen.

The truth in the statement that you cannot like or love anyone else until you like and love yourself brings truth and relevance to many situations, but none more so than when it comes to being able to commit to a relationship. This is true because you cannot give to someone what you do not have to give.

If you do not have a self you like and love, you cannot expect anyone else to do so. So go ahead...give yourself the freedom to like and love the wonderful, amazing, unique and talented being you are.

REMEMBER: Relationships depend on your self-confidence because...

You must have confidence in order to begin a relationship

You must have confidence to be able to say no to unhealthy relationships

You must have confidence in order to commit to a relationship

Relationships are connections

You must like and love yourself if you expect others to do the same

You deserve happy, healthy relationships

STUDY NOTES

"
A Man stands in his own shadow and wonders why it's dark.

~Zen Proverb

Why Self-Confidence Matters: Careers

How many times do you think you were asked what you wanted to be when you grew up? Too many to count, right?

When you were asked that question, what was your answer? More importantly, what type of response did you get to your answer? Were you encouraged? Did people make comments like, "That's great!" "I can see where you would be good at that." "I'm sure your parents will be proud of you." or "Don't forget about me when you are rich and famous."

Or, did you hear things like "Are you sure you can do that?" "You don't have the grades to make it into medical school (or whatever)." "It's nice to dream, but you'd better choose something more realistic." "What makes you think you can do that?" "You may as well forget it. People like us don't do things like that."?

Chances are you get a little of both—both positive and negative feedback. That's normal. Unfortunately, sometimes it only takes one negative response to damage your self-confidence to the point of letting go of your hopes and dreams for your future. This CANNOT be!

You cannot let the opinions of others bring you down. Nor can you let someone's opinions decide your future for you. Instead, you need to trust your own thoughts and interests and the guidance of those who have your best interests at heart to make you confident enough to pursue your goals and dreams...no matter what.

I was the kid everyone smiled at, patted on the shoulder and said, "That's nice." When I told them I wanted to be a teacher. First of all, people in my tiny town barely graduated high school, much less go on to college. Secondly, I was born with a heart defect that required three surgeries by the time I was six and I am deaf in one ear. So when I said anything about going to college, you could feel the patronization take over the room.

Thankfully my parents didn't feel that way. They said they knew there was nothing I couldn't do—that I'd proved that over and over again. After my high school graduation I went to state university with scholarships enough to pay everything for at least the first two years.

I've been teaching fourth grade for three years now...to the children and grandchildren of the very same people who said I would never make it. –Maggie

Sadly, not everyone has the support system Maggie did. Sadly, some people (maybe even you) let the negativity of others win out over the voices in their own hearts and minds. This is what happened to Isaac...

Isaac loves football. He has since he was just a little kid. He knows the history of the game, game stats, rules and calls.... It's not hard to understand why his nickname is Mr. Football. It also comes as no surprise to anyone that knows Isaac that he wants to pursue a career revolving around the sport. Few people believe it will happen, though, because Isaac is only 5' 3" and barely weighs 200 pounds.

I know I don't have a future playing football. I don't even play on my high school team. Instead, I'm a manager and the first student coach ever. I'm okay with that. I just wish everyone else was, too. My parents don't even come to the games. They say I'm wasting my time—that I should be thinking about something that matters and that I can actually do.

I try to tell them that I plan to major in physical education and provide a recreational football team for kids like me—kids too small to play on a sanctioned team. They just laugh. Maybe it is a stupid idea. Maybe, but if it is, why can't I quit thinking about it? Stupid or not, I know I owe it to myself to try. –Isaac

Maggie and Isaac both have goals and dreams. Maggie has achieved one of her greatest goals, while Isaac is still trying to navigate the road to his. Maggie has people on her side who have cheered her on and who have helped her in whatever ways are necessary and possible. Isaac doesn't have the support system he deserves and needs. But Isaac has the confidence in himself and his abilities to keep going in spite of everything and everyone.

What about you? Do you believe in what you want to do? Do you believe in yourself enough to be the little engine that can instead of giving up and giving in? If so, keep going. Stay focused on what it is you want to do and go after it with all you've got; doing what needs to be done to help you reach your career goal. If not, things need to change. You need to:

- Find someone who believes in you and share your dreams and goals with them; asking for their moral support and to hold you accountable for doing what needs to be done.

- Assess your goals and dreams. Are they realistic? For example: Is your dream to become a doctor, yet you cannot stand the site of blood or refuse to visit someone in the hospital because hospitals 'creep you out'?

- Are you preparing yourself to meet your goals? Are you confidently pouring yourself into your education in order to make the necessary grades and to develop the study habits necessary to prepare you for college?

- Are you confident enough in your goals and dreams to remain outside the box people are trying to put or keep you in?

The need for confidence in making career choices and decisions doesn't stop with choosing if or where to go to college and with deciding what to do with your life. No, the need for confidence continues throughout your entire career. Possessing a strong self-confidence allows you to:

- Take calculated risks for furthering your career

- Be noticed by your superiors when it is promotion time

- Stand up for yourself in a professional manner when you are being taken advantage of

- Earn the respect and trust of your co-workers

At this point in your life you are just beginning to formulate a plan for your future career. You are exploring avenues of interest and deciding how to incorporate your passions and interests into something you can actually earn a living doing. The process isn't always an easy one, is it? It can, however, be a whole lot easier if you go through the process with confidence in who you are and with the confidence that you can do anything you set your mind to. The sky really is the limit!

REMEMBER: Being confident...

- **Lays the foundation for fulfilling your goals and dreams**

- **Should not be dependent upon the thoughts and opinions of others when it comes to making career choices**

- **Gives you the strength and courage you need to ignore negativity**

- **Makes you a prime candidate for scholarships, promotions and other career-related accolades**

- **Makes you someone who gets respected and noticed by co-workers**

STUDY NOTES

If you want to be happy, be.

~Leo Tolstoy

Why Self-Confidence Matters: Happiness

Another way to word Tolstoy's comment is to say that happiness is a state of mind—not something you get or achieve.

Do you understand what that means? It means happiness is something that comes from within and is only possible when you allow it to be.

Because happiness is an attitude or state of mind, it is fair to say that you cannot really experience happiness unless you are confident in who you are and what you have to offer.

This doesn't mean you never have doubts about the choices you make or that you never feel unsure or even intimidated by situations you find yourself in. What it *does* mean, though, is that the choices and situations will not dictate your overall outlook on life.

The confidence you have in yourself and who you are will override any feelings you have of being unworthy of being happy. When you stop and think about it, happiness and self-confidence are pretty much interchangeable.

The confidence that comes from being happy gives you the courage and will to express your opinions, act on your ideas and to go after your hopes and dreams. When you do, the happiness that comes from being yourself practically oozes out of you. Combine that with the sense accomplishment you feel from being yourself and your self-confidence grows. When it does, you stretch yourself, set bigger goals (and go after them) and on and on the cycle goes.

Or you can choose to sit back and let life happen all around you; blaming other people and your circumstances for holding you back and making you miserable. Laying blame instead of taking responsibility is a real happiness killer, though. In fact, it is impossible for you to be happy or self-confident when you hand control of your thoughts, feelings and emotions over to someone or something else.

This leads to another cycle—one moving in the complete opposite direction of the one we described earlier. *This cycle is laying blame for your circumstances, living in denial of your responsibility, feeling miserable and worthless then laying blame for feeling worthless and miserable, which leads to more negative situations which leads to....* You get the picture.

Crystal was your average teen-ager. She and her family weren't rich, but they weren't poor, either. Her mom had always stayed home with her and her two younger brothers.

Her dad was a VP in a bank in their small town. Crystal was a good student and involved in choir and volleyball. She was friendly and outgoing and looking forward to graduating and going to college to become an elementary teacher. Yes, Crystal was happy and confident in who she was and where she was headed...or so she thought.

Half-way through Crystal's senior year in high school, her dad admitted he had gotten into financial trouble because of a bad investment. He'd even spent her college fund trying to recover some of the money.

She was furious and convinced her life was completely ruined. She blamed her father for ruining her future and stealing her chance to achieve her goals. She was angry and resentful and withdrew from her family and friends.

It wasn't until Crystal's mom and aunt firmly, but lovingly told Crystal it was time to quit feeling sorry for herself and get on with living life. They agreed that what her father had done was unfair to her and deceptive and damaging to their entire family.

But they also reminded Crystal that while what had happened could not be changed, she had a choice. She could either let her father's poor choices be the catalyst for her poor choices or she could continue to be her smart, positive, enthusiastic self and take responsibility for her future instead of handing it over to her situation.

It hasn't been easy, but Crystal is about to take semester finals for the first time. She ended up going to a less expensive college, but one that offered her a volleyball scholarship and some academic scholarships. This will allow her to graduate with very little student loan debt. She is still not on good terms with her dad but she is finally feeling confident and happy again about who she is instead of blaming her dad for what and where she isn't.

So you see, no matter what your situation, it all comes down to you. Man or Woman, YOU are the one controlling how you feel and what you think. YOU and you alone have the power to be happily self-confident and confidently happy with who you are.

- **Remember...to be happy**
- **Be thankful for all things big and small**
- **Be resourceful; finding positive ways to make things happen**
- **Be optimistic; finding the good in every situation**
- **Look in the mirror each day and like who you see**
- **Don't be afraid to show yourself to others; using your natural talents and abilities to do life**

- **Go after what makes you feel fulfilled and complete**

- **Surround yourself with the people you love and who value you**

- **Laugh**

- **Do for others instead of always doing for you**

- **Decide what you think and how you feel and don't allow others to take that from you**

Happiness and self-confidence do go hand in hand, but both are great assets to have, so what's so bad about that? Absolutely nothing!

STUDY NOTES

SECTION (3)
WHY CONFIDENCE MATTERS

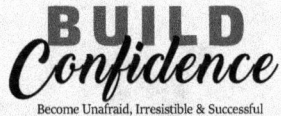

> Always be
> a first-rate
> version of
> yourself, instead
> of a second-rate
> version of
> somebody else.

~Judy Garland

How To Be Confident: Like Yourself

Everything you do—from breathing and moving to homework and hanging with your friends is an action you choose to take. And with all those actions come consequences. Some consequences are good, some are bad and some are indifferent, but there is always a consequence.

Okay, you say, that's true enough, but what does that have to do with self-confidence? A lot.

Your actions and the consequences of your actions tell the story of how you feel about yourself. People who feel good about themselves make better choices than people who don't. People who feel good about themselves are also more successful because they are more confident about what they are capable of. We know this is true because:

25% of teenage girls say they would like to have plastic surgery to change something about their appearance.

A girl's self-confidence begins to drop after she has her 10th birthday.

90% of teenage girls are more afraid of being fat than they are of losing their parents or of our country being attacked by nuclear weapons or of dying in a car crash.

Nearly 15% of teenage boys take steroids to bulk up to look 'better'.

Three-fourths of teenagers asked say they don't feel they are good enough in some way (looks, grades, relationships, have enough money, sports, popularity....)

One out of every three teenagers is overweight or obese. Much of this is due to poor diet and supervision of how to eat properly, but once the weight begins to add up, food becomes a comfort and safety net, which then leads to more weight gain which leads to lower self-confidence and on it goes.

As you read those statistics, how closely can you identify with any or all of them? Chances are you fall or fell into at least two of those groups.

What's more, the ones that don't describe you describe at least one of your friends. The question, though, is why? WHY don't you like yourself? WHY aren't you confident that you are special and unique and have something good and positive to offer to those around you and to society in general?

For some of you the answer to that question would be that you've never been told just how great you are. Instead, you are made to feel like you are just in the way...

Maxwell was only four when his parents divorced. He hasn't seen his dad since the day he left. He didn't even say goodbye. What's worse is that Maxwell heard him tell his mom that they (Maxwell and his mom) were tying him down.

Maxwell is fourteen now and still believes he was the reason his dad left. He doesn't understand that his leaving was his choice—that he and his mother were not the cause of his leaving. But because Maxwell sees himself as nothing more than an obstacle in his dad's life, he does whatever he thinks is right in the moment to make someone want him.

He has been sexually active for over a year, had a girl have an abortion a few months ago and steals from his mom and grandma to give and sell things to other kids so they will like him. What Maxwell doesn't realize, though, is that none of these kids like him. They are only using him. But then why should they like Maxwell when he doesn't even like himself?

Maxwell is his own worst enemy when it comes to being self-confident and successful in life. While it's true he is the 'victim' of a bad parent, most of Maxwell's problems are self-inflicted because he only sees himself from his dad's perspective. There's no denying Maxwell's pain is real and that hearing a parent say they are leaving because you are in the way of their happiness is harmful to your sense of self-worth.

But Maxwell cannot continue to punish himself for something he did not do. If he does, there won't be any room in Maxwell's life for confidence and happiness.

Maxwell's situation isn't fair to him and that's sad. But life is not fair and you have to be able to look past all of that to see yourselves for the person you really are and LOVE the person staring back at you in the mirror. You have to quit believing the lies others tell and start listening to the truth inside your head and your heart.

Believing you are in the way is just one reason people have trouble liking themselves, though. Other reasons include:

1. falling for the media's unrealistic expectations and portrayal of what is good, sexy, pretty and even normal.

2. being shy and unwilling to let people see who you are and what you are capable of, and

3. being made fun of or even bullied; making you feel there really is something wrong with you.

Learning to like yourself and to be confident that being yourself is enough may not be easy—especially if you've not been shown how special you are in the past. Don't let this stop you, though, because without taking this all-important first step, self-confidence is impossible.

Learning to like yourself is the key to a life of confidence and happiness and happens when you:

- Accept yourself. Look in the mirror and accept the occasional zit or two or three, the bad hair days, the nose you think is too big or too small, the freckles and the body that isn't magazine perfect. FYI: What you see in the magazines is courtesy of the touch-up software.

- Forget about being perfect and just give your best. Your best may not always be *the* best, but as long as it is always *your* best, that's all anyone has a right to expect from you.

- Don't compare yourself to others and don't allow yourself to be compared to others by someone else. You and you and that's enough. This isn't to say you shouldn't stretch yourself to learn more, take chances and experience new things.

- Just be sure you are doing these things to better yourself because it is what YOU know is best for you—not because you are trying to live up to someone else's expectations.

- Learn the difference between being alone and being lonely and understand it's good to spend some time alone. To be alone is to spend time by yourself. Spending time alone is quiet time without interruption. To be lonely is to be left out of activities and conversations with your peers. Loneliness is not having anyone to confide in and depend on. Remember...being alone from time to time is NOT a bad thing.

Spending time alone:

- Gives you the privacy you want to be honest with your feelings
- Allows you to concentrate on studying and homework
- Allows you to dream and set goals on your own terms
- Gives you the quiet and space you need and want to form opinions and deal with emotions.

The flip-side; Yes, The Other Side

Numbers don't lie; meaning it is impossible to ignore the fact that so many teenagers are having trouble with confidence and positive self-esteem. But there is always a flip-side to everything and in this case it is pride and feeling superior—like you are better than others and more deserving because you are you.

We all know someone (or a few someones) like that. These are the kids (and adults) who expect and even demand attention, recognition and special treatment because they feel entitled or that it is owed to them because of their last name, their status in the community, their abilities or sometimes just because they *want* it.

I have noticed in the 20 plus years I have provided counseling, that many parents thought spoiling their children was showing love, unfortunately for many of these children entitlement becomes their down fall when they are not able to receive the same nurturing and attention.

At first glance people like this are often admired or respected for their self-confident nature. But it usually doesn't take long for you to find out that what you thought was self-confidence is really bragging and boasting.

It's one thing to put yourself out there to use your abilities to take you where you want to go in life and to accept recognition for what you have accomplished. It is another thing, though, to *expect* your abilities and your accomplishments to always be center-stage and to overshadow everyone else's. Do you see the difference?

When all is said and done, you have to be able to like—even love—who you see staring back at you in the mirror before you can expect anyone else to be able to like and love you. You have to lead the way to your heart and to your mind.

- **Remember…liking yourself means you:**
- **Accept yourself for who you are**
- **Don't compare yourself to others**
- **Always keep striving to be your best**
- **Don't expect perfection because it doesn't exist**
- **Know that being yourself is all anyone has a right to expect of you**
- **Taking responsibility that how your life turns out is all about you and your choices**
- **The world and everyone around it, including your parents do not owe you anything, you owe you everything…its all up to you what you decide to do with this one life**

STUDY NOTES

"Education and learning increases your confidence level. By giving yourself a chance to learn, you increase your and desire to be self-confident"

~Dr. Stem

How To Be Confident
Take Care Of Your Mind

Back in the sixties and early seventies, everywhere you turned you heard or saw the phrase, "A mind is a terrible thing to waste". You see, at this point in time, college was considered to be just one of many options for your future rather than the assumed path for the high school graduate.

There were several reasons for this push toward high education:

1. The war in Viet Nam was coming to an end and a lot of people wanted nothing to do with our military.

2. The civil rights movement was still fairly new, so there were lots of doors opening to black students that only some had been able to pass through before.

3. The drug culture in our country was HUGE! Addiction to heroine and other drugs was running rampant. Deaths due to overdosing on drugs were a common everyday occurrence everywhere. People needed to know there was more to life than going down that dark and dead-end path.

4. Young soldiers coming back from Viet Nam were suffering from PTSD but could get no help, so turned to alcohol and/or suicide for relief.

5. We were just entering the age of technology. We needed sharp, educated thinkers to take us where we wanted to go...where we are today.

All you have to do we had to do was ask our parents, watch a few old television shows or walk through a flea market or antique shop to see how far we've come. But one thing that hasn't changed (and never will) is the value of challenging your mind by reading, learning and discovering new things.

It's true not every school has the same opportunities to learn and experience new things. And it's true that some students fall through the cracks because of learning disabilities and difficulties they have to deal with outside of school (abuse, homelessness, poverty, etc.).

But as long as you are in school you have the opportunity to learn something and when you don't take advantage of these opportunities you aren't hurting anyone but YOURSELF.

If you don't learn to read past a third grade level you are the one who is going to pay for that by not being able to fill out a job application, graduate from high school so you can go on to college and a career.

Even for adult not reading, taking courses to enhance yourself will keep you stagnant in one miserable boring place.

If you don't concentrate on learning the basics of math you are the one who will struggle with knowing how to manage money, plan and stick to a budget, know when people are taking advantage of your (ripping you off), knowing how much you should pay for something, how to figure out where you are going and how long it will take to get there and all sorts of common everyday life skills you need.

If you don't know how to spell, write and punctuate correctly, you are the one whose job applications will get tossed in the trash. Why would anyone want to hire someone who cannot even communicate in their own language?

If you don't grasp the concepts of science and how things work, you will be the one who doesn't understand how their body works, how to make things grow, why you shouldn't stick your finger in an electrical outlet and why electricity and water don't work well together.

If you refuse to see history as important, you will not understand why and how we have the freedoms we have, the importance of voting and why we need to support and respect those who serve in our military.

If you do not take every opportunity to learn and do your best in school, you are the one who will stop you from being the banker, teacher, doctor, business owner, mechanic, or fashion designer you want to be.

While it is more difficult to learn when you are facing homelessness, hunger, abuse and being in a school where the teachers either don't care or don't have the resources to teach the way they want to, it is NOT impossible to clear these hurdles. If you WANT to do something you CAN because you have the POWER inside of you to be CONFIDENT and SUCCESSFUL.

Clearing the hurdles:

- Libraries are public buildings where anyone can go to read, study, check out books and use the internet.

- Most communities have after-school programs to keep you out of trouble, offer you a snack (or meal) and a warm, dry, safe place to do your homework and grow your skills. You may go to a church, a community building or even your school to participate, but these things are out there for YOU. Just ask someone at your school. They will know.

- Ask for help. The first place you should start is with your teacher. When you give them attitude and send the message that their class is the last place you want to be, it's hard for them to get excited about their job. But when show them you are interested in what they have to say, you will be surprised at just how much they really do care.

- Tell someone. If you are being abused, if you are hungry, if you are having trouble hearing or seeing or understanding what is being taught, tell someone. Tell your parents (if they will listen). Tell your school counselor. Tell the person in charge of the after school program. Tell your teacher. Tell someone and keep on telling until someone listens and gets you the help you deserve.

- Believe and don't give up. No matter where you live, how much money you do or don't have, what color your skin is, the size and shape of your body, how your parents treat you or how many friends you have, YOU can be anything you want to be. BUT (don't you just hate it when there's a 'but') YOU are the only one who can give yourself the confidence that comes from learning.

Think about it...don't you feel better about yourself when you understand what a discussion is about? Don't you feel better about yourself when you do well on a test? Don't you feel better about yourself when you finish something you start? Yes you do!

These things don't just happen, though. They happen because you make them happen for yourself when you decide to love learning.

So when school gets you down or you feel like you can't keep going or that learning something is a waste of time, remember that to use your mind for learning is opening the door to a life of confidence and success.

There's one more think you need to remember. You need to remember that learning doesn't just happen in the classroom. Learning happens:

- When you read—books, newspapers, magazines and the internet

- When you play sports—learning the rules of the game and the value of good sportsmanship and teamwork

- When you have friends—learning how to be socially appropriate, how to share, make and keep promises, be trustworthy and do for others

- When you have a job—learning to follow instructions, respect authority, handle criticism, work as a team, be on time and focus on the jobs you are given to do

- When you do things—science projects, hobbies, musical instruments or other artistic interests

- When you spend time with people older and wiser than you who are a positive influence on you

- When you set goals for yourself and work to achieve them

"A mind is a terrible thing to waste"— the saying may be an old one, but it definitely falls under the category of 'oldie but goodie'.

- **Remember...learning helps with confidence**

- **Learning is the key to success**

- **There are always opportunities to learn if you will take them**

- **Learning disabilities don't have to stop you from learning**

- **Help is available if you ask for it and take it**

- **Learning doesn't just happen at school**

- **Believe you can and deserve to learn**

"Our choices show that we truly are far more than our abilities"

Ralph Waldo Emerson

How To Be Confident
Take care Of Your Body

Have you ever watched a bird with an injured wing try to fly? Or have you ever tried to tie your shoe with just one hand? Or think about how you feel the first day back at school after having the flu or a cold. It's hard to be who you are supposed to be and do everything you are supposed to do if your body isn't cooperating, isn't it?

Our bodies have 206 bones, 640 muscles, 10 trillion cells, 13 major organs and 65 other organs. Each bone, muscle, cell and organ has a job of its own, but when even one part of the body isn't working properly the rest of the body is thrown off balance. We don't always notice or feel the difference, but it is there and if nothing is done to bring the body back into balance, our bodies can break down even more.

Body breakdown facts

- Body breakdowns can be as minor as a case of the sniffles or chapped lips or something more serious like a heart attack or being overweight or obese.

- Some body breakdowns can't be avoided. Everyone gets a cold or the flu at least a few times in their lives. Some diseases are hereditary. Heart attacks happen to people who seem perfectly healthy. Cancer can happen to anyone.

- Some body breakdowns don't have to happen. All you have to do is take care of yourself.

- Body breakdowns can make you feel self-conscious instead of self-confident. When you don't feel good or like the way you look, you start doubting your ability and your self-worth.

Believe it or not, all those things your mom has been telling you about taking care of yourself are right! Taking care of your body is directly linked to your self-confidence, your ability to achieve your goals and how you interact with other people.

We know this is true because of the statistics like the ones we looked at in a previous chapter. Statistics that show:

- 45% of teenage girls either starve or purge themselves on a regular basis in order to lose weight.

- Anorexia is the third most common chronic illness in girls between the ages of 10 and 25.

- 69% of girls between the ages of 10 and 18 say they depend upon magazines and other media to tell them how they should look and dress.

- Over 80% of children over the age of 10 are afraid of being fat.

- Over 50% of teenage girls and 35% of teenage admit to doing unhealthy things to their bodies to try to lose weight.

Do you realize what these statistics are saying? They are saying that you and almost every one you know are responsible for putting your body in breakdown mode. These statistics also show that the things you and your peers are doing in order to feel better aren't working. If these things did work, the number of teens suffering from anxiety and depression wouldn't be on the rise.

Are you beginning to see the connection between your body and self-confidence? Are you beginning to have a better understanding of how important it is to take care of your body so that you can be confident and happy with yourself?

Of all the things you can do to increase your level of self-confidence and your ability to be 'loud and proud' about who you are (in a good way), taking care of your body is one of the easiest things you can do. It is easy because there is so much information and help available to help you—including the encouragement and suggestions listed below:

- Eat a healthy diet. There's a reason junk food is called junk. The fresher something is, the better it is for your body. Stay away from foods with chemicals, dyes, sugars and fats that don't come from nuts and dairy foods. The body is designed to process natural foods. Processed, chemical-laden foods (including diet soda) are hard for the body to break down and process. These foods confuse the body and cause it to make and store more fat and cause damage to some of the body's organs.

- Get up and move! Twenty minutes a day of exercise is all it takes IF combined with a healthy diet to start dropping pounds to be a healthier you. Of if your weight is fine and you want to stay that way, the same diet and exercise plan will work for you. It is also a good idea to move around for at least two or three minutes an hour.

- Practice good hygiene. Daily showers, brushing and flossing your teeth and washing your face with something to help prevent acne aren't really optional. When smell, look and feel clean you are more confident.

- Don't abuse your body. Alcohol, tobacco and drugs are all harmful to your bodies in more ways than one. Not only do these things have a negative effect on the body's organs, but they are also addictive.

- This means a body becomes dependent or convinces itself that it needs these things to function. Addiction is a dangerous illness that robs a person of their self-respect, confidence and hope for a happy and successful future.

- Don't harm your body. Cutting, eating disorders and other forms of self-deprecation are symptoms of having no self-confidence or sense of self-worth. Doing things like this to your body is saying you do not like or value yourself.

- Take pride in your appearance. Clean hair, clothes that are neat, clean and fit well are important for feeling confident.

- Smile and laugh. Having a positive attitude is proven to make you feel better about yourself and life in general.

- A healthy body is a happy body and a happy and healthy body is a body you can be proud of and confident in.

Remember: A healthy body...

- **Is your responsibility**

- **Happens when you eat a healthy diet, get exercise, do nothing to harm or abuse your body and take pride in your appearance**

- **Gives you a clear mind**

- **Is the impression you make on others**

- **Gives you the courage and strength to achieve your goals and dreams**

STUDY NOTES

He who trims himself to suit everyone will soon whittle himself away

~Raymond Hull

How To Be Confident: Toss Your Weaknesses In The Trash And Walk Away Fast

Have you ever signed up for something because your best friend did—even though you really didn't want to? Maybe they wanted to play in the school band but you didn't know the difference between a saxophone and a clarinet. What happened? Ding! Ding! Ding! I know! I know! Your friend had a blast and ended up in first chair, but you were miserable and spent most of your time just pretending to play the notes and listening to the teacher's constant mantra of "You may not think music is your thing, but it can be if you want it to be". Or...

Have you ever gone out for a sport you don't like or aren't suited for because your parents are so sure "You can do it if you try"?

While your parents and teachers usually mean well, it is time for you to know that it is more than okay to say no to trying to be something and someone you aren't. It is okay to admit you aren't cut out to do something and move on instead of wasting time better spent on being the best possible YOU. Whew! What a relief, right?

Know when to hold 'em and know when to fold 'em (lyrics from Kenny Roger's song "The Gamble"

Fact: Hundreds, if not thousands of books have been written on the subject of overcoming your weaknesses and turning your weaknesses into strengths.

Fact: The subject matter of these books is counterproductive and a waste of time and energy (no disrespect intended).

Fact: Some things are just not meant to be.

Fact: Trying to overcome your weaknesses instead of concentrating on your strengths is a confidence stealer.

If the slipper doesn't fit, it just doesn't fit

Cinderella's stepsisters wanted to be the one whose foot fit the dainty little glass slipper and become princess. They pushed and strained and tried with all their might to get the slipper on their not-so-dainty feet. But we all know both attempts failed. It wasn't even close.

That's the way it is for all of us. We all have our glass slippers; things we will never do or achieve or become for no other reason than we just don't fit. And you wanna know what? That's okay.

- Trying to be or do something you aren't cut out to be or do is such a waste of time, energy and self-confidence. It's like digging the hole even deeper when you spin your wheels trying to get out.

- **Weakness you are trying to overcome**

Feeling frustrated, unhappy or bored

Doing poorly or failing

Feeling like a failure, decreased self-confidence

Wishing you were doing something else

Trying again and again because that's what everyone says you are supposed to do

It's a It's a continuous and depressing cycle that is easy to get sucked into if you don't

- Know what your strengths and weaknesses are
- Believe it is okay to let your weaknesses go and concentrate on your strengths
- Take control of your own future and quit trying to fit into a shoe that won't fit no matter what you do

It was obvious why the slipper didn't fit either one of Cinderella's stepsisters. It's not always as easy as that to know or accept our weaknesses—especially if it is something we really want to do. That's why it is so important to know both your strengths and weaknesses so you will know where your focus needs to be in order for you to be confident, fulfilled and happy. To help you do that, answer the following questions:

1- How do you enjoy spending your spare time?

2- What are your favorite things to do?

3- Where are your favorite places to go?

4- Do you enjoy spending time by yourself?

5- Would you rather learn something new by watching, listening or using your hands?

6- What are your favorite subjects in school? Why?

7- If you could choose any career, what would it be?

8- What subjects in school do you dislike and struggle with?

9- What careers are the biggest turn-off to you?

10- What do YOU think your strengths and weaknesses are?

This little quiz isn't meant to be a definitive personality assessment, but your answers to these questions will help you realize what your strengths and weaknesses are and how to use this knowledge to be the best, most confident you possible.

NOTE: *Acknowledging your weaknesses does not give you permission to ignore obligations. For example, if math class is something you struggle with, you still have the responsibility to do your personal best instead of throwing in the towel because it is a weakness. But it also means you need to avoid careers that require strong math skills.*

The most excellent you

Alex was living and loving the life of a happy, healthy sixteen year-old. He had a great relationship with his parents, he made B's and C's in school and was one of two sophomores to play varsity on football. That all changed on Friday night when he took a hit and in the matter of seconds was paralyzed from the chest down.

Days and weeks and months went by with Alex going to therapy session after therapy session. He put his heart and soul into getting stronger and to regaining even the smallest amount of feeling and use of his body. He tried to be polite and positive when people told him over and over and over that they 'just knew' he would get better or when they cautioned him to not give up. It wasn't easy, though, and there were days when Alex just wanted to feel sorry for himself for the rest of his life. But that's not who Alex is. Alex knows that he is never going to walk again—much less play football.

Alex knows that the exercises he does won't produce a miracle, but will allow him to learn how to do a few things for himself. Alex knows his mind is still as clear and capable as it was before the accident and that this is now the strength he must focus his energies on. If he doesn't, Alex knows he will spend his life being bitter and angry and feeling worthless.

Alex's circumstances are extreme, to say the least, but fundamentally they are no different from yours. No matter what other people say or think, you can only be the person you are made to be.

Each of us has natural talents and abilities; those things that just click with us and make us feel accomplished, complete, fulfilled, confident and all those other good things we like to feel.

But when we are coerced or forced or guilted into, or even made to believe we should be doing something we're not suited for, we are trying to accomplish the impossible. This isn't to say you can never put paint on a brush and swipe it across the paper, but there's a big difference between painting a stick figure and the Mona Lisa.

Do you understand what is being said here? Do you understand that fulfillment, happiness and confidence come from realizing your strengths and running the distance with them instead of wasting your time trying to overcome your weaknesses?

But shouldn't I try?

Great question. Why shouldn't you try to turn your weaknesses into strengths? To answer that question think about the things you dislike doing the most. Do you have those in mind? Okay, now think about being told you will be required to spend eight hours a day doing those things a) until you like them and are really good at doing them or b) for the rest of your life—whichever comes first.

How would you feel? Exactly.

Now think about the things you enjoy doing most—the things you are good at. Do you have those in mind? It wouldn't be nearly as hard to hear you were going to be doing these things for the rest of your life, would it? In fact, the thought of being able to do what you love doing all day, every day make you feel excited. You know before you begin you will be successful and your confidence level is soaring.

Now do you see why it is a waste of time to try turning your weaknesses into strengths?

That being said, you should be willing to try new things and stretch yourself and your abilities, but if doing something makes you feel bad about yourself and it is obvious you are not cut out to do this thing, then fulfill your obligation to the best of your ability and move on with a clear conscience.

Remember: Concentrating on your strengths instead of your weaknesses…

- **Gives you confidence**

- **Makes for a more fulfilling life**

- **Doesn't remove you from the responsibility of always doing your best**

- **Shouldn't be used as an excuse to not try something new**

- **Will allow you to contribute to relationships and society in a more positive way**

STUDY NOTES

> A machine has value only as it produces more than it consumes — so check your value to the community.
>
> ~Martin H. Fischer

How To Be Confident: Dare To Show You Care

If you were taken to the opening of a cave, handed a flashlight and instructed to find your way the other end of the cave to rescue your best friend, what would you do with the flashlight? Would you stick it in your pocket? Throw it down so you would have two free hands? Use it to knock debris out of the way? Hold it out in front of you to feel for obstacles in your way? Or would you use the light to its full potential by turning it on so you could use its light to help you find your friend?

Well, duh, you say. That's a dumb question. Maybe, but how often do you ignore or pass up opportunities to help other people? How often do you keep your light turned off when you could be leading the way?

Ouch! That's not nearly as fun to think about as picturing someone stumbling around in a cave with a turned off flashlight in their hands, is it? Sorry, but at this point in your life you need to be searching out opportunities to contribute to society and to help others by offering your talents and resources to make life better for someone else.

The fact that you can work independently, make good choices based upon the facts and your knowledge of right and wrong, are old enough to mentor younger children and provide assistance to older people and are capable of learning to be aware of your surroundings makes you a prime candidate for community volunteerism and service.

Why should you care

    *It's better to give than to receive

    *Do unto others as you would have them do unto you

    *You reap what you sow

    *What you give is what you get

    *Pay it forward and it will come back to you

    *A life well spent is worth more than all the money in the world

    *Investing in others is more valuable than money

These are just a few of the wise old sayings we hear about the importance and benefits that come when we dare to care about someone else. Take another look at them. As you do, think about the people who have dared to care about you. Who are they? Why do you think they take the time to love, help and care for you?

Do you deserve the things they do for you? Do you ever express your appreciation for what they do? How do you express your appreciation?

Being on the receiving end of someone's kindness is pretty nice, isn't it? It makes you feel like you matter and that you have value as an individual.

So in case you still need an answer to the question of why you should care, you should care because someone cares about you. You should care because it is the right thing to do. You should care because caring for one another is what makes society work.

There's one more reason you should dare to care and that reason is YOU. You should dare to care about others because in doing so, you become more confident in who you are and your ability to contribute to society in a positive and productive manner.

When you take the time to put yourself out there and offer yourself for the good of someone else you are acknowledging the fact that you can be of benefit to others. This isn't meant to make your service to others sound prideful to imply you should do for others in order to draw attention to yourself. Not at all!

The point being made here is that when you serve and care for other people you experience a degree of confidence and satisfaction in yourself emotionally, mentally and sometimes even physically (I really did help build that house for Habitat for Humanity). These feelings then allow you to become even more confident and in tune to who you are and what you have to offer, which then leads to being confident enough in yourself to do and become more.

Not always a happy ending

Being on the receiving end of someone's help doesn't always create a warm, fuzzy feeling. Sometimes people become defensive, embarrassed and even resentful. They have a difficult time admitting they have a need.

When this happens, the person offering the help sometimes comes away feeling rejected, misunderstood and hurt. An experience like this can even lead to someone being afraid to help or even cynical about offering someone a helping hand.

This is sad and unfortunate, but when or if this happens to you, you need to remember that sometimes when people are hurting, they put up defenses in an attempt to not get hurt worse than they already are.

Think of it like this: a wounded dog will often bite the hands of the people trying to help. The dog isn't biting because he doesn't want help; he is biting because he's afraid there is going to be more pain.

If you get your feelings hurt by trying to help someone who won't accept your help, it is important to walk away from the situation with the confidence that you tried to do the right thing. Remember...you cannot make someone take your help.

Caring requires sacrifice

When you dare to care about someone besides yourself, you are saying you are willing to put your own wants and needs aside for the sake of someone else. Sacrificing your wants and needs for those of someone else may require nothing more than letting them in front of you in the lunch line or letting you little sister have the last of the ice cream in the freezer.

But there are times when daring to care about others will require you to give up activities and things you want, care about and maybe even need so that someone else's needs and wants will be met. The question is how much are you willing to give up for someone else?

There is no one right answer to that question. Some of you have more to give up than others do. Some of you are naturally more generous than others. No matter where you are right now, though, one of the objectives of this course is that you decide to grow in your willingness and ability to dare to care for others.

No, it won't always work out the way you may have envisioned it, and no, you won't always get a pat on the back and a 'way to go!'. But if you dare to care about someone for the sole purpose of helping and showing compassion, then no matter what the results are, you will always gain a bit of confidence in knowing you are not afraid to do the right thing.

Remember: Daring to care...

- **Isn't about attention and recognition**
- **Doesn't always make things good**
- **Isn't always welcome**
- **Is always the right thing to do**
- **Builds confidence**
- **Should be done out of love and concern for someone**

SECTION (4)
WHAT HAPPENS WHEN YOU ARE CONFIDENT

"
Sometimes
the difference
between a successful
person and one who
isn't is confidence to
believe in one's
abilities and inner
strength

~DrStem

What Happens When You Are Confident: Self-acceptance

So your nose is a little crooked and your hair is a color you describe as muddy brown. So you don't have six-pack abs and you bench less than any other guy in gym class. So everyone knows your dad can't or won't hold a job and you share a room with all three of your siblings. So you aren't perfect. No big deal, because nobody else is, either!

A little over a year ago Target® was targeted (pun intended) in a new report that revealed they were air brushing and manipulating their advertising photographs to make the models in these pictures skinnier, 'perfectly' proportioned and with flawless skin tone and facial features. But oops! They got a little carried away and moved arms where they couldn't be, forgot to follow through on some of the photo cropping and as a result, they put out ads with somewhat humorous mistakes.

This incident (along with a few others like it) has spawned a small but growing number of magazines and websites who are using real people who wear real sizes who eat real food and have real lives in their advertisements and articles.

Finally, the media is beginning to recognize the harm they have caused to people (especially children and teenagers) by presenting a false perception of what it means to be healthy, pretty, sexy, friend-worthy and successful.

When you are confident in who you are and what you are capable of, you are proof that what the media is just now figuring out has been right all along and always will be. When you are confident in yourself, you are saying:

- You know you aren't perfect, but that you are perfectly happy with who you are

- You are worth far more than even the most expensive designer jeans or purse

- You have something to offer no amount of photo shopping or cropping can make better

- You know your strengths and weaknesses but have decided to focus on your strengths

- You don't need to change who you are to suit the needs and wants of others

- You believe being you is all anyone has a right to expect of you

- You know that the confidence that comes from accepting yourself for who you are is valuable to you and to everyone around you.

Don't confuse self-acceptance with arrogance

- The confidence that comes from self-acceptance should never be confused with arrogance. The confidence with self-acceptance is not a license for treating others as if they are less valuable than you, to look down on others because they have less than you do, or do not have the same strengths as you do. The confidence that comes from self-acceptance does not give you the right to make demands, act selfishly and/or insist on things being done your way. These behaviors are not displays of self-confidence. They are displays of arrogance and insecurity.

Remember: Self-acceptance is...

- **Essential for living a life of confidence and fulfillment**

- **Loving yourself and loving others for who they are**

- **NOT insisting on having your way**

- **NOT looking down on others—seeing them as less important**

- **Being happy with who you are and making the most of who you are.**

The will
to win, the desire to
succeed, the urge to
reach your full
potential...
these are the keys that
will unlock the
door to personal
excellence.

~Confucius

What Happens When You Are Confident: Rising To The Challenge Of Setting And Meeting Goals

When you are confident you view a challenge as something to be accepted and conquered—not something to run from.

When you are confident you view a challenge as something that will help you grow into a better you—not something to blame for holding you back.

When you are confident you view a challenge as something to show yourself and others what you are made of—not something to humiliate and embarrass you.

When you are confident you set goals for the purpose of having the life you desire to have.

When you are confident you don't see goals as a set-up for failure.

When you are confident your goals are a roadmap of sorts to keep you focused.

When you are confident your goals are realistic yet get you out of your comfort zone to expand your abilities.

Goals...who needs them

What is a goal? A goal is defined as a plan of action to reach or achieve a desired result. In other words, it's the plan you follow for getting things done.

Goals keep us focused. Goals also help us avoid mistakes and provide direction. Ultimately, though, making and achieving goals allows us to feel accomplished and confident.

Callie's parents believe in teaching their children to be responsible and to have a strong work ethic. This means Callie and her brother and sisters have chores to do. It also means that if they want a car when they turn sixteen, they have to buy it.

Callie started saving money for a car when she was fourteen. She saved a part of all the money she got for her birthday and money she earned babysitting, doing extra chores around the house and helping some older people clean their houses. Callie set a goal to save $1,500 in two years. She knew she needed to save an average of $15 a week for almost two years to meet that goal.

Some weeks she was able to put $30 in her car account and some weeks she couldn't put anything, but when she turned sixteen, Callie had $1,560.

There were times when I wanted to spend part of my car money for other things, but I didn't. There were also times when I could have put more in my car account than I did but spent the money on other things. I just had to make sure I averaged $15 a week. I'm really proud of myself for doing it. It shows me that I can manage money when I have a real job and have to pay rent and stuff like that. I'm also really proud of my car. It's nothing fancy, but it's mine and that's a really good feeling. ~Callie

The confidence that comes with setting and achieving goals serves to encourage you to keep going. Goals are, in many ways, the fuel feeding the little engine saying "I think I can. I think I can. I KNOW I can."

Remember: Setting and achieving goals...
- **Keeps you focused**
- **Helps you avoid mistakes**
- **Builds confidence in your abilities**
- **Encourages you to get outside of your comfort zone**
- **Brings results**
- **Helps you see when and where things go wrong**
- **Allows you to accomplish more**

The will to win, the desire to succeed, the urge to reach your full potential...these are the keys that will unlock the door to personal excellence.

~Grandma Moses

What Happens When You Are Confident: Life Looks Good And The Future Looks Bright

In case you haven't noticed, this course is about giving you the tools and inspiration you need to be confident in who you are and what you are capable of. Ultimately, though, the choice is yours. No matter how many pages are in this book or how many quotes are quoted to cheer you on, if *you* don't make the choice to like yourself and to be confident in who you are and what you are capable of, this book and all it contains is worthless.

It all comes down to that one word-confidence. Confidence is at the root or foundation of seeing life as a glass that is half-full and waiting to be filled to the brim instead of half-empty and waiting to be knocked over and spilled on the counter.

*Confidence allows your smile to come from the inside out.

*Confidence gives you the strength and courage to keep going when it would be easier to stop or turn around and go back to where you started.

* Confidence is being able to laugh at yourself when you do something funny.

* Confidence is knowing you don't always have to be right.

* Confidence is being happy for others when they win.

* Confidence is knowing life isn't fair but wanting to give it all you've got anyway.

* Confidence is moving in the right direction for you even if you are swimming upstream in the expectations of others.

Joey had every reason to see life as half-empty. His parents left the distinct impression that being a parent was an inconvenience to them. When he and his sister turned seventeen they were given the option of paying room and board for being allowed to live at home or being legally emancipated. Being emancipated would require them to move out and be totally self-sufficient.

Joey chose to be emancipated. He moved into a tiny hole of an apartment next to the high school and worked two afterschool jobs to make his way. It wasn't easy, but Joey was confident he could make it. So when he graduated with a 3.4 GPA, he was proud of what he'd been able to accomplish and looked forward to college.

There was just one problem—his parents.

The FAFSA would not acknowledge Joey's emancipation and required his parent's tax return information to award him any PELL Grant funding. They refused to provide the information saying they did not want to be tied to any student loan or grant issues. Joey was upset, but knew there was nothing he could do about it.

So instead of letting this destroy his confidence and his dreams, Joey worked two jobs to save all the money he could possibly save. The semester before he turned twenty-one (as an adult he wouldn't need his parent's information for PELL Grant funding), he enrolled in college and was able to pay for his first two years with grant money and the money he had saved.

Today Joey is a college graduate, happily married and is the father of a baby boy. Joey refused to let anyone or anything destroy his confidence in himself to have a happy, fulfilling future.

Having the confidence in yourself to decide to be happy and enjoy life no matter happens and no matter what or who tries to convince you to do otherwise is a 100% guarantee for a life well lived. So you see, Grandma Moses knew exactly what she was talking about when she said life is what we make of it.

But then, aren't grandmas always right?

Remember: Confidence affects your life and your future...

- **By giving you courage to go after your dream**

- **By giving you hope**

- **By giving you purpose**

- **By reassuring you that no one can take your confidence from you unless you let them**

STUDY NOTES

If you don't manage your emotions, your emotions will manage you.

~Doc Childre

What Happens When You Are Confident: You Have Control Of Your Emotions

Emotions are the feelings you have because of your mood, your circumstances or your surroundings.

Some people cry when they are sad. Others withdraw from everyone. Some people express anger by throwing things. Other people yell when they get mad. Some people laugh when they get nervous and others break out in a sweat and can't find their voice. The emotions are the same in everyone. It's the reaction to the emotion that varies.

Why do people express emotion differently? The answer to that is best summed up by saying it is a matter of personality. Some people are more sentimental than others. Some people are more patient than others. Some don't cry watching a sad movie. Other people need a box of tissues for sentimental commercials.

The fact that we all have emotions and that we all express emotions differently won't make us smarter or better or nicer or weaker or harsher than someone else. It is how we manage or control our emotions that matters.

How to manage your emotions

*Recognize your emotions. If you are sad, be sad. If you are excited, be excited. If you are nervous, be nervous.

*Know what triggers your emotions.

*Limit your exposure to things that cause negative emotions.

*Consider your options for dealing with emotions in a more positive manner.

*Think before you speak and act out of emotion. Will what you say or do be helpful or harmful to you and to others?

*Decide to manage your emotions instead of letting them manage you.

What happens when you manage your emotions

When you are confident in who you are and what you are capable of, it is easier for you to deal with or manage your emotions because you are more aware of who you are and not afraid to express yourself appropriately. As a result, you become even more confident when you see the positive effects that come from being in control of your emotions.

- People respect someone who is in control of their emotions

- You have healthier relationships when you are in control of your emotions

- You make better choices when you are in control of your emotions

- People who are in control of their emotions are healthier and happier than those who aren't

Remember: Confidence brings self-control...

- **To help you recognize your emotions**

- **To give you the strength to deal with your emotions appropriately**

- **To encourage you to avoid negative emotional triggers**

- **To express emotion in a healthy and mature manner**

"

It is the mark of an educated mind to be able to entertain a thought without accepting it.

"

~Aristotle

What Happens When You Are Confident: Your Education Matters

This quote by Aristotle could very well have been the basis for country song popular back in the early 2000's that contained the words, "You've gotta stand for something or you'll fall for anything".

Do you understand the message in these words and in Aristotle's quote? The message is that if you aren't confident in who you are and your ability to express yourself and make decisions, you will end up being told what to think, where to go and what to do with your life.

But that's not all Aristotle is saying. Aristotle is also saying that the educated mind is able to listen to another person's point of view respectfully even if they do not agree or accept what is being said.

This kind of confidence doesn't just happen, though. This kind of confidence is only possible when you take every opportunity to learn. Think about it…if you don't listen to the news you cannot have an opinion of what is going on in the world because you don't *know* what's going on.

If you don't learn all you can in reading and grammar classes, you will not have the skills necessary to fill out a job application or have the skills necessary to understand rental agreements, loan agreements or even directions on how to put something together. In other words...the confidence that comes from having an education matters.

To further prove this point, statistics show that:

- Every single day in this country, over 8,000 kids drop out of high school. That adds up to over 3 million high school dropouts per year.

- Those 3 million kids make up less than 20% of the general population, but...

- Those 3 million are responsible for 75% of the crimes committed in our country.

- The fact that they do not have a high school diploma makes them ineligible for 90% of the jobs available.

- These statistics are additional proof that the confidence that comes from having an education matters.

- The confidence that comes from having an education allows you to:

- Express your opinions without feeling ignorant

- Think for yourself

- Stand up to peer pressure, bullying and people who try to tear you down
- · Experience countless opportunities that will allow you to achieve your goals and dreams
- · Make positive contributions to society

Everyone needs a high school education if they want a future that is not bleak, depressing and immersed in poverty, dependency and low self-esteem. Beyond high school, the options are wide and varied. For some, trade schools and technical colleges are the road to success. For others, more academic styles of learning are desired and required.

The amount and extent of your post high school education will depend upon the career choices you make. Each type of education is valuable and important—it takes all kinds of people and professions to make this world go 'round. What d*oes* matter, though, is that you go as far as you can go and achieve all you can achieve in your desired career so that you will have the confidence in yourself to know that you bring value and positive contributions to your family, friends, co-workers and to society as a whole.

Remember: Education matters because...

- **It gives you the confidence to express your thoughts and opinions**

- It gives you courage to stand up to peer pressure, bullying and those who try to tear you down

- It gives you opportunities to achieve your goals and dreams

- It gives you confidence to participate and contribute to society

SECTION (5)
YOUR CONFIDENCE IN ACTION

Make the most of yourself, for that is all there is of you.

~Ralph Waldo Emerson

Be Confident: Show The World Who You Are

Confidence. How many times have you read and heard that word throughout the time it has taken to complete this course? A lot—to say the least. That's okay, though, because you are worth it. You are worth every bit of time, effort and energy it takes to convince you that you have the ability to become everything you want to be if *you* believe you can.

Throughout this book you have discovered how to achieve a strong sense of self-confidence and the value that comes for doing so. But just like holding the key to a brand new car that is sitting in your driveway will do you no good unless you put the key in the ignition and take it out for a spin, your self-confidence is worthless until you show the world who you are and what you are made of.

The final chapter of the workbook you've been using gives you three options for a final project. Each of these options is designed to take the tools you've been given and put them to good use. Each project will require you to exhibit your self-confidence physically, emotionally and mentally. Choose the project that most appeals to you and run with it. As you will see, there are few guidelines. This is about letting you show the world what an amazing person you are and what you are capable of.

So...get ready...get set...GO!

Self Confidence Affirmations

Self-confidence affirmations, when repeated again and again, along with counseling and coaching, will help you build self-confidence.

But what is self-confidence? Self-confidence is nothing but self-assuredness in one's behavior, ability, etc. It is the belief of believing in yourself, to believe that one can accomplish what one sets out to do, to overcome obstacles and challenges.

Your perception of yourself has an enormous impact on how others perceive you. Also, the more self-confidence you have, the more likely you are to succeed.

- I deserve to be happy and successful.
- I have the power to change myself.
- I can forgive and understand others and their motives.
- I can make my own choices and decisions.
- I am free to choose to live as I wish and to give priority to my desires.
- I can choose happiness whenever I wish no matter what my circumstances
- I am flexible and open to change in every aspect of my life
- I act with confidence having a general plan and accept plans are open to alteration
- It is enough to have done my best
- I deserve to be loved
- I love meeting strangers and approach them with boldness and enthusiasm.
- I am self-reliant, creative and persistent in whatever I do.
- I love change and easily adjust myself to new situations.
- I always see only the good in others. I attract only positive people.

- When I breath, I inhale confidence and exhale timidity.
- I love meeting strangers and approach them with boldness and enthusiasm.
- I approve of myself and love myself deeply and completely.
- I live in the present and am confident of the future.
- My personality exudes confidence.
- I am bold and outgoing.
- I am self-reliant, creative and persistent in whatever I do.
- I am energetic and enthusiastic.
  Confidence is my second nature.
- I always attract only the best of circumstances and the best positive people in my life.
- I am a problem solver. I focus on solutions and always find the best solution.
- I love change and easily adjust myself to new situations.
- I love challenges. They bring out the best in me.
- I am well groomed, healthy and full of confidnce.
- My outer well being is matched by my inner well

being.

- Self confidence is what I thrive on.
- Nothing is impossible and life is great.
- I always see only the good in others. I attract only positive people.
- I face difficult situations with courage and conviction. I always find a way out of such situations.

Add more of your own:

_____

_____

_____

_____

_____

_____

Unshakable Self-Confidence Workbook

EXCERCISE ONE:
● LITTLE THINGS MATTER

I am so excited about this section because I believe the ultimate confidence comes from Becoming a Successful person in all aspects of your life. To become successful I have learned that you have to answer a lot of questions, I mean a lot of questions so that you can be crystal clear about who you are, what you want and what you are capable of becoming and creating. Sometimes one message, one question can make all the difference in your life. I believe :You can create any life you want, no matter how difficult it may seem, by understanding how small, positive steps make a difference over time. It's the things you do every day that don't even seem to matter... that do matter most.

I encourage you to use this Workbook to fully apply the new self -confident you to become unstoppable, create the best life that you deserve and live a happier stress free life. Upon completing the questions in the workbook, You will come to understand that little things do matter, your thoughts matter, what you say matters, the choices you make are important, and yes, you can make your dreams come true, I did.

What Does Success Mean To You?

What does success mean to you? To find out, start with these questions:

- What's important to you?
- What do you like to do?
- What do you care about?
- What things mean the most to you?

After you've thought a while, jot down your thoughts in the spaces below.

What are five things you're good at? List them here:

_____

_____

_____

_____

_____

Now, what are five things you love to do, whether or not you're especially good at them? (You may end up listing some or all of the same things in your first list. That's OK.)

1 _____

2 _____

3 _____

4 _____

5 _____

And now, let's take it a step further, too: What are five things you would do if you could, no matter how outrageous they are, even if you think you're no good at them?

_____

_____

_____

_____

_____

And now, let's take it a step further, too: What are five things you would do if you could, no matter how outrageous they are, even if you think you're no good at them?

_____

_____

_____

_____

_____

_____

This gives you a pretty good idea of how you define success. But how are you going to get there? By taking small steps. So, let's take the next step.

Success Starts with Little Steps

Think of three little things you can do that could lead to success in six areas of your life. Then write them down below. (Remember—they can be small steps! And you can repeat what you've written above in the spaces below.)

For Myself

1 _____

2 _____

3 _____

For My Friendships

1 _____

2 _____

3 _____

For My health (physical, mental, and spiritual):

1 _____
2 _____
3 _____

For My Wealth:

1 _____
2 _____
3 _____

For My Education and career:

1 _____
2 _____
3 _____

For My Footprint on the World (what I want to accomplish or how I want to be remembered):

1 _____
2 _____
3 _____

Which of these steps can you take today?

_____

_____

_____

_____

_____

Excercise 2:
Attitude Is Everything

What is your life Philosophy?

If you could sum up in a few sentences how you see yourself and the world, what would you say?

- Are you pleased with the way you see yourself? Are there things you want to change?
- What about the way you see the world? Is it a welcoming place or a scary one? Or neither?

However you see it, write it down here.

Here's how I see myself:

_____

_____

_____

_____

_____

_____

And here's how I see the world:

_____

_____

_____

_____

_____

_____

Now, think about what you just wrote. Why do you think you see yourself and the world that way? Where did your philosophy come from? Write your thoughts below.

_____

_____

_____

_____

_____

_____

_____

_____

Are you pleased with what you wrote? Surprised? Saddened? Anything you'd like to change? Write your reactions here.

_____

_____

_____

_____

_____

_____

_____

_____

Maybe you're happy with what you've written. Maybe not. If not, that's OK—at least you know what needs to be changed. Whatever your philosophy looks like, the key to getting what you want, to creating your dream life, is to make your philosophy work for you and not against you.

Success Key: If You Want to change Your Life, change Your Philosophy

But before you can use your philosophy to your full advantage, you have to know what parts of it are working for you and what parts are holding you back. Let's find out.

What parts of your philosophy are helping you achieve success? Jot down your answer below.

_____
_____
_____
_____
_____
_____
_____

Now, think about what parts of your philosophy don't work so well. Are there ways of seeing the world or yourself that are holding you back or causing problems in your life? Write your answer here.

_____
_____
_____
_____
_____
_____
_____

How Do You Talk to Yourself?

How you think has a big effect on how you live your life.

Try to remember a time when you were successful at something that was new or really hard. What did you say to yourself after you accomplished it? Whatever it was, try to remember it and jot it down here

_____

_____

_____

_____

_____

Now, think back to a time when you tried to do something really hard and didn't do well. Can you remember what you told yourself? Write it down here.

_____

_____

_____

_____

_____

_____

_____

_____

_____

_____

Did you give yourself credit for succeeding and believe you could do it again? Or were you very hard on yourself and not confident about succeeding?

Now think about your philosophy and the way you think. Then answer these questions:

How are your philosophy and the way you think related to each other?

_____

_____

_____

_____

_____

_____

Are your philosophy and way of thinking mostly positive or negative? For example, do you expect the worst or best from people? Do you tend to put yourself down?

_____

_____

_____

_____

How would you like to change your philosophy and the way you think?

_____

_____

_____

_____

_____

_____

_____

_____

STUDY NOTES

Exercise 3
There's Power in this Moment

Past or Future?

Let's try an experiment to show you two different ways your mind works. Really do this—it's fun, pretty fascinating, and will take just a few minutes.

First, take a comfortable, seated position and look down at the floor, at a spot right between your toes. Take a few deep breaths, and then, staying in that position, take the next two minutes or so to think about your life. Anything and everything in your life—it doesn't matter what, just whatever comes to mind.

All right? Go!

What did you think about? Jot it down here.

_____

_____

_____

_____

_____

_____

_____

_____

Now, clear your mind, get up and walk around for a minute, then come back and do the second half of the experiment.

This time, take that same comfortable, seated position, only tilt your head up so that you're looking at the ceiling. Take a few deep breaths, and then think about your life over the next two minutes or so—again, it doesn't matter exactly what you think about, just focus on whatever comes to mind.

All set? Go!

What did you think about this time? Jot it down here.

_____

_____

_____

_____

_____

_____

_____

Now, how did those two experiences compare? Did you think about pretty much the same things both times, or were they different?

For example, during the first part of the experiment, did you find yourself thinking about the past? Did any regrets come to mind? Did you find yourself thinking about things you could have or should have done differently?

During the second part, when you were looking up at the ceiling, did you find yourself thinking about the future? Were your thoughts and feelings more positive?

If so, you're not alone. Most people find it's pretty hard to not start thinking about the past when looking down. And when looking up, it's hard not to think forward into the future, about hopes, ambitions, and aspirations. It just seems to come naturally.

The point is this: Looking behind you will cause you to feel and act much differently than if you look to the future (and make plans to make it the best).

a Look in the Mirror:

How do you view your present circumstances—your family, school, friends, neighborhood, and state of mind? What's going well? What's holding you back?

Think about each part of your life listed below. For each, do you tend to see yourself as at the mercy of what happens (not taking action), or someone who is in charge of what happens (ready to take action)? Be as honest as you can with this—and if you don't like any of your answers, don't worry: We're going to show you how to change them!

For Myself:

_____
_____
_____
_____
_____
_____

For My Friendships:

_____
_____
_____

For My Friendships:

For My Health (physical, mental, spiritual):

_____

_____

_____

_____

_____

For My Wealth:

_____

_____

_____

_____

_____

_____

For My Education and career:

_____

_____

_____

_____

_____

_____

For My Footprint on the World (what I want to accomplish or how I want to be remembered):

_____

_____

_____

_____

_____

_____

Perhaps this exercise helped you see where you need to take action. Lots of times we wait for a lucky break. But good things will happen if you start to take little steps to achieve your goals.

So let's start taking those steps.

STUDY NOTES

Exercise 4
Everything Starts With Small Steps

The Power of Small Steps

Think about something you had to do in the past that seemed impossible—a project at school, saying sorry to a friend, or participating in a sporting or outdoor event. It should be something that you thought you couldn't accomplish but did.

Describe how you felt when you first thought about tackling this big thing in your life.

_____
_____
_____
_____
_____
_____
_____

Now, looking back, think about the small steps you took to tackle this challenge and how you felt afterward. Describe those steps and feelings here.

_____
_____
_____
_____
_____
_____

After it was over, did the challenge seem as hard as it did at first? Did you get the confidence to tackle other hard challenges? Did you give yourself credit for succeeding?

_____
_____
_____
_____
_____
_____

a Single Step You can Take

Previously, I asked you to describe three steps you could take in each area of your life to reach your goals. Now you can narrow it down even further—what is one simple thing you can do in the next 24 hours that would help you reach your goals in the following areas (just one thing).

Have fun with this—be creative!

For Myself:

_____
_____
_____
_____
_____
_____

For My Friendships:

_____
_____
_____
_____
_____
_____

For My health (physical, mental, and spiritual):

_____
_____
_____
_____
_____
_____
_____

For My Wealth:

_____
_____
_____
_____
_____
_____
_____

For My Education and career:

_____
_____

_____

_____

_____

_____

For My Footprint on the World (what I want to accomplish or how I want to be remembered):

_____

_____

_____

_____

_____

_____

_____

Hold on to your ideas. When we get to the last exercise, you'll start using them. (But if you want to put them into action right now—go ahead!)

STUDY NOTES

Exercise 5
There's No Such Thing As Failure

The Key TO Success is Failure

Let's look at your own life. Think back to something you failed at (or thought you failed at). It could be a test in school, the first time you tried a new sport, or anything else that didn't go as you expected.

Describe what happened here.

_____
_____
_____
_____
_____
_____
_____
_____
_____
_____

Think for a moment about what you've written and answer this question: What did you learn from that experience? Did anything positive come out of it, no matter how small? Write your answer here.

_____

_____

_____

_____

_____

_____

Now ask yourself: What did I learn from this experience that I can use in the future? What can I do differently next time, either in the same situation or a different situation? Write it down here.

_____

_____

_____

_____

_____

Do you look at your "failure" in a different way? Do you see positive ways to use "failure" in the future? Jot down your thoughts.

STUDY NOTES

Exercise 6
Habits Are Powerful

What Are Your Habits?

Think about the habits you have. Don't judge whether they're good or bad habits—that's not the point right now. Merely describe below the habits you have in doing your schoolwork, relating to friends, deciding what to wear or eat, what music to listen to, or in any other area of your life.

_____

_____

_____

_____

_____

_____

Now, are there any habits you want to change? Again, don't judge them or put yourself down. Just list below the habits you'd like to try to change.

Starting new habits

Reflect on changes you'd like to make in your life. But forget about changing old habits. Instead, what new habit or habits can you start in each area of your life?

New habits I can start for myself:

New habits I can start with my friends:

_____

_____

_____

_____

_____

_____

New habits I can start for my health (physical, mental, and spiritual):

_____

_____

_____

_____

_____

_____

New habits I can start for my wealth:

_____

New habits I can start for my education and career:

New habits I can start for my impact on the world (my accomplishments or how I will be remembered):

_____

_____

_____

_____

_____

_____

_____

Which new habit would you like to start first? Can you start it today?

_____

_____

_____

_____

_____

_____

_____

STUDY NOTES

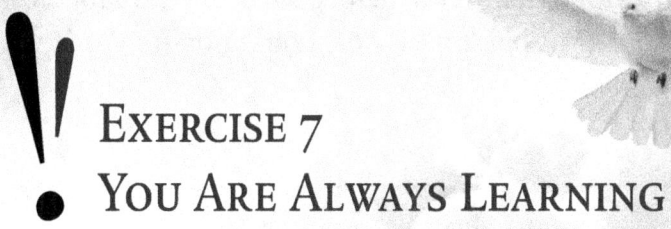

Exercise 7
You Are Always Learning

Always Take Advantage of Opportunities

What new skills or new opportunities would you like to have? Jot down your thoughts here.

_____

_____

_____

_____

_____

_____

_____

Find a Mentor

A mentor is an adult who can help you learn a skill or gain a certain kind of knowledge.

Is there an adult who can help you achieve what you want? Who is that person? What would you like to learn from him or her?

_____

_____

_____

_____

_____

Adjust Your life course, life plans

Are there ways you need to "adjust course" in your life—to change the way you see things or do things? What are they?

_____

_____

_____

_____

_____

What steps could you take to adjust your life course, your life plans?

STUDY NOTES

Exercise 8
Make Your Dreams Come True

Make Your Dreams Into Reality

To reach the specific and tangible goals that make up success, there are four steps you need to follow.

- You must picture it vividly.

- You must look at it every day.

- Understand and pay the price.

- Start with a plan.

Picture It vividly

Choose a dream you have, any dream—an accomplishment, a triumph, your dream house, dream car, dream job, the relationship of your dreams. Look back at the answers that you wrote after each exer- cise. Keep choosing until you have five dreams.

Jot them down here...

My Five Dreams

1. _____
2. _____
3. _____
4. _____
5. _____

My Five Dreams in More Detail

Rewrite the same five dreams below, only this time add whatever words you need to make each one as specific as possible. Picture it vividly—and make that picture real and here and now.

1. _____
_____
_____
_____
_____
_____
_____

2.

3.

4.

_____

_____

_____

_____

_____

5. _____

_____

_____

_____

_____

_____

When Will You accomplish Your Dreams?

The next question is, "By when?" In the spaces below, write out each of those five dreams one more time, this time adding words that answer the question.

"By when?"

I Will accomplish My Five Dreams by...

1. _____

_____

_____

_____

2. _____

_____

_____

_____

3. _____

_____

_____

_____

4. _____

_____

_____

_____

5. _____
_____
_____
_____

Create a Dream board

Another way to make your dream vivid is to find a bunch of pictures that represent the things you want to accomplish and make them into a collage. You can cut pictures out of magazines, print them off the Internet, or take photos of things you want. Use the pages here to create your "dream board."

Look at It Every Day

In the space below, write out a list of declarations that you can say to yourself every day about each of your five dreams.

My Dream Declarations:

1. _____
_____
_____
_____
_____

2.

3.

4.

5.

Start with a Plan

You have to start with a plan. Whatever you can dream, you can do. So do it! Write out your plan for each dream below, being as specific as you can.

My Plan for reaching My Dreams

1. _____
_____
_____
_____
_____
_____

2. _____
_____
_____
_____
_____
_____

3.

4.

5.

Small Steps I can Take Every Day to reach My Dreams

Think about your five dreams. Now, for each dream, think of small steps you can take each day to begin making them come true.

1. _____

_____

_____

_____

_____

_____

_____

2. _____

_____

_____

_____

_____

_____

_____

3.

4.

5.

> Now, start pursuing your dreams today!
>
> CONGRATULATIONS
>
> You have moved yourself to the TOP 2% of people who are Successful.

Join the Empowerment Academy for more:

Encouragement
Empowerment
Inspiration
Motivation
Confidence Boost

Telephone and Video COACHING

I Enjoy Providing Online Telephone and Video Coaching & Counseling Services For Adults, Teens, College Students, Couples via Phone, Facetime, Whatsapp, skype and Zoom.

I Offer Free 30 Min Consult Session and Affordable Coaching/Counseling Packages which are listed under coaching Tabs on my website, www.drstemmie.com.

Reserve Your Free Consult Session on
https://www.drstemempowerment.com
Or

You can also Contact me for more info at drstem14@gmail.com or whatsapp at (781) 254-1602

Let's Connect

Join Dr. Stem on Face Book Live on Tuesday evenings for discussions on topics discussed in this book and more.

Enroll in Teen Empowerment Webinars and online courses, and connect with other teenagers around the world for moral support, fun and encouragement. All online programs are on:
https://www.drstemmie.com/

Look out for the Parent & Teen Empowerment Conference or Workshop coming to your city, a city near you or at sea. Inquire at
drstem14@gmail.com

About The Author

Originally from Zimbabwe, Southern Africa, **Dr. Sithembile "Stem"Mahlatini** is president and owner of **Global Counseling & Coaching Services,** in Orlando, Florida, and she is also president and founder of Parent & Teen Empowerment Conference & Parent & Teen Empowerment Seminars.

She is a certified life-career coach, author, licensed psychotherapist and motivational/inspirational speaker. She resides in Orlando, Florida USA.

Dr. Stem's life's work is to inspire, motivate and educate others through her books, seminars, workshops, and Counseling and Coaching Services.

Drawing on her background as a licensed psychotherapist, life- career coach, speaker and author, she offers people practical advice on how to tap into their limitless power to change their lives, overcome roadblocks and aspire to be better than the circumstances that surround them.

Her life-long goal is to continue to empower and inspire teenagers, parents, and couples to be winners at home, work and business.

Her motto is, "Each day is an opportunity to change your life and bring out the new you."

Dr. Mahlatini attended Nova Southeastern University where she earned a doctorate degree in education, specializing in organizational leadership. She is also a graduate of Boston University, where she earned a master's degree in social work, and she is licensed as a psychotherapist in Massachusetts and Florida.

She is a member of the Back Talk Toastmasters club, the Professional Woman Network, and the National Association of Social Workers.

Listen on The DrStem Show Podcast on Spotify

Watch DrStem on The DrStem Show on Youtube for inspiration, encouragement and motivation through the interviews she conducts on the show,

https://www.youtube.com/results?search_query=drstem+show

In addition to speaking and training, she counsels and coaches clients in her private practice offices in Altamonte Springs, Skype and telephonically. She serves clientele throughout the United States, Africa, the Caribbean, the United Kingdom, and Australia through one-on-one telephone coaching services.

Dr. Stem is available as a trainer and speaker for onsite trainings, groups, and one- on-one coaching for parents, teenagers, women and organizations. Consultations are conducted by telephone or on-site. Her programs include:

- Bridging the Gap Between Parents and Teenagers
- Pampering The "Princess Within"
- Overcoming Being All Things to All People
- Possibilities – Turning Dreams into Reality
- Free at Last – Setting Boundaries
- How to Deal with Toxic People
- 15 Strategies to Achieve Your Dream
- How to Live a Simpler Life
- Living a New Life of Confidence- Developing A Healthy Self Esteem
- Taking Charge of Your Life, Money and Family
- Change Your Thinking – Change Your Life
- The Rollercoaster Ride Is Over! Handling Emotions
- Handling Stress: Sink, Swim or Float & MoreBook

Dr. Stem Mahlatini as your next motivational/ inspirational speaker for your women's retreat, church, youth retreat, seminar, school assembly, or Business Management–Employee event.

MORE BOOKS BY DR STEM

Books Authored and Co-Authored by Dr. Stem On:

http://www.amazon.com

http://www.pwnbooks.com/order.htm

http://www.walmart.com

1. Unstoppable- Living a Free and Fearless Life
2. Thriving Beyond the Tears- Bruised But never Broken
3. Parenting Teens Q & A
4. Teen Girls Q & A
5. Teen Boys Q & A
6. It's Time To Shift From Fear To Faith
7. Surviving College-Dealing with studies, stress, depression, suicide, drugs and more
8. 47 1/2 things to say to your teen and how to say them
9. 47 1/2 things teenagers need to know about their parents
10. CDC-Courage Determination Confidence Teenager's handbook to socially acceptable life skills
11. Build Confidence achieve Success
12. Profits are better than wages -key to living your dreams
13. Confident not Corky -why self esteem is key to success
14. The blessings of being a woman

15. 365 Daily success & motivation doses for teens
16. 50 a celebration of life lessons
17. Dose of motivation & encouragement for teachers
18. Zero Limits – A teenagers guide to life choices
19. Zero Limits – A teenager's guide to life choices (Christian)
20. The power of prayer and belief
21. Finding your true self-bringing clarity & purpose to your life
22. Unstoppable - A woman's guide to self confidence
23. Build Confidence Become Unstoppable
24. Respect- connecting with disconnected students Co Author
25. Beyond the scars - Real Life Accounts Of Women Who Overcame Adversity Co author
26. Success within Reach: Reconditioning your paradigm Co author
27. Emotional Wellness For Women Vol I Co-Author
28. Emotional Wellness For Women Vol II Co-Author
29. Emotional wellness For Women Vol III Co-Author
30. Celebration of Life: Inspiration for Women Co-Author
31. How to Survive When Your Ship is Sinking: Weathering Life's Storms Co-Author
32. The Baby Boomer's Handbook for Women Co – Author

REMEMBER

After reading this book, I look forward to hearing your story and how you were able to boldly make decisions that have changed your life for the better. Email me at drstem14@gmail.com

If you would like me to interview you on my radio show The DrStem Show

https://americaoutloud.com/show/the-drstem-show/

Email me at drstem@americaoutloud.com

You Matter

Your Life Matters

You Are Unstoppable

To Your Success, Be Unstoppable!

Dr. Stem, Be Encouraged

STUDY NOTES

www.ingramcontent.com/pod-product-compliance
Lightning Source LLC
Chambersburg PA
CBHW071233080526
44587CB00013BA/1596